MOOD
✦ JOURNAL ✦

This journal belongs to

__Pamela Canales__

__2024__

Contents

6
HOW TO USE THIS JOURNAL

✦ INTRODUCTION ✦

10
THE IMPORTANCE OF SLEEP

·

12
HOW FOOD AFFECTS YOUR MOOD

·

14
WHY PHYSICAL HEALTH MATTERS

·

16
WHY MENTAL HEALTH MATTERS

·

18
MENSTRUAL HEALTH AND MOODS

·

20
BALANCE YOUR SOCIAL LIFE

·

22
WEATHER AND MOODS

✦ JOURNAL ✦

26
MONTH ONE

40
MONTH TWO

54
MONTH THREE

68
MONTH FOUR

82
MONTH FIVE

96
MONTH SIX

110
MONTH SEVEN

124
MONTH EIGHT

138
MONTH NINE

152
MONTH TEN

166
MONTH ELEVEN

180
MONTH TWELVE

HOW TO USE THIS JOURNAL

✦ ✳ ✦

Many factors influence our moods on a daily basis. Sometimes a combination of things might put us in a good mood; at other times it could be one small factor that makes us feel low or irritable. When reflecting on our moods, it's important to consider the whole picture, and the activities in this journal will enable you to do just that. You'll have space to record information on your sleep, diet, physical health, mental health, menstrual health and how sociable you are, and look at how these factors affect your mood. Be sure to analyse your recordings alongside each other, not in isolation. You might notice interesting patterns that will enable you to make small changes to improve your moods.

MONTHLY OVERVIEW

The 'monthly overview' at the start of each month is a great place to reflect on the month as a whole. There's space for you to write notes, which you could do as you go along throughout the month, or you might prefer to summarise at the end of the month. Perhaps you'd like to include something here about anything significant that's been happening – maybe you've been going through a difficult time, or maybe you want to expand on why you've had a particularly positive few weeks.

There's also a calendar for you to complete, and it's useful to do this every day so you don't lose track and forget how you've been feeling. You'll need some colouring pencils! Look at the coloured emojis on the calendar pages and shade each day in the relevant colour(s) depending on how your mood has been. See the example on the following page.

Remember you can use more than one colour on each day. There's also space for you to quickly jot down what the weather has been like, whether you've done any exercise and whether you've socialised. You'll have the opportunity to record more about exercise and sociability later on in the month, but this provides at-a-glance information to help you identify any patterns. It's up to you how much detail you want to write – you could write 'sunny' for the weather or alternatively draw a sun; you could write 'yes' against exercise or be more specific with something like '5K run'; and when you record whether you've been sociable you could write a person's name who you saw that day or simply include a tick.

MENSTRUAL HEALTH

Most of the journal pages are self-explanatory or include instructions/suggestions on how to complete them. When you get to the 'menstrual health' section, which obviously won't apply to everyone, refer back to this diagram for help on how to complete it. It's a great way to track your cycle and identify patterns in your mood.

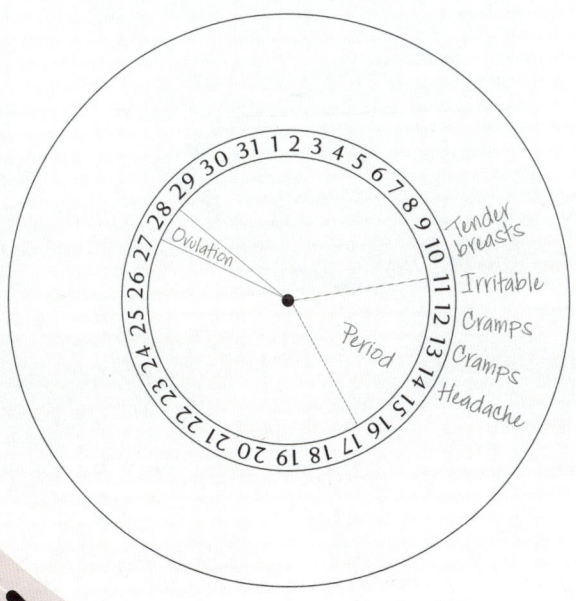

7

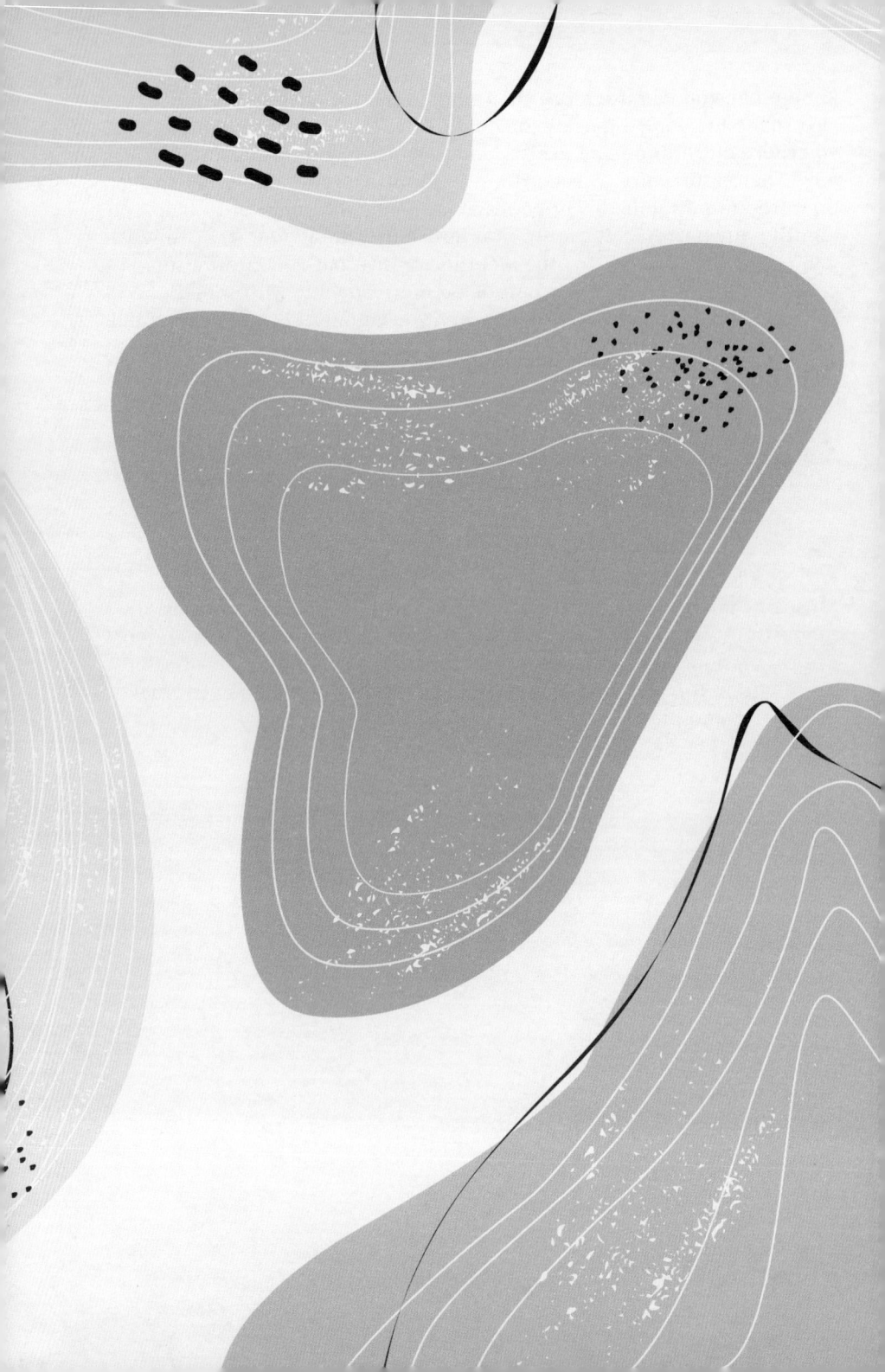

INTRODUCTION

10
THE IMPORTANCE OF SLEEP

12
HOW FOOD AFFECTS YOUR MOOD

14
WHY PHYSICAL HEALTH MATTERS

16
WHY MENTAL HEALTH MATTERS

18
MENSTRUAL HEALTH AND MOODS

20
BALANCE YOUR SOCIAL LIFE

22
WEATHER AND MOODS

THE IMPORTANCE OF SLEEP

Sleep accounts for about a third of our day and is one of the biggest factors when it comes to our moods

✦ ✷ ✦

Sleep is one of the foundations of a balanced mood, and yet it can sometimes get overlooked with our busy lives. Long gone are the days when we could sleep in a natural rhythm with the seasons. Work, children, socialising and entertainment all impinge on our sleep patterns.

The odd sleepless night isn't going to do you too much harm – it's often easy enough to get an early night the next day and catch up for lost hours. However, if you're consistently getting less sleep than you need, you will build up a sleep debt that's much harder to compensate for.

There has been a lot of research on the link between sleep and negative mood. If

DISCONNECT FROM TECH

The blue light from your phone and smart devices can suppress melatonin, the hormone that helps us sleep. Disconnect at least half an hour before bedtime to help improve your sleep.

you're sleep-deprived on a long-term basis, then you're likely to feel angry, irritable and upset. It also means you're less likely to be able to make decisions, focus on tasks or enjoy activities, which can also contribute to a low mood. A lack of sleep can also make you feel less sociable and less likely to engage in things you enjoy, impacting on your relationships and hobbies.

The average healthy adult needs around seven to nine hours a night. However, we're all different and each of us will have our own sleep requirements. Every day is different too – sometimes you need more sleep, depending on what you've done. Our bodies are pretty good at telling us if we've had enough sleep – if you wake up feeling tired, groggy or in a low mood, then you haven't had enough.

Conversely, it's also possible to have too much sleep. If you've stayed in bed too long, you might wake up feeling a bit groggy and fuzzy-headed, and this can also impact negatively on your mood. This is why it's important to be consistent with your sleep patterns – going to bed and getting up at the same time every day. If you can find the right timings for you, where you wake feeling positive and balanced, you will experience an uplift in your mood. Once you have this routine in place, you will find you can cope with the odd disruption and late night – simply fall back into your usual sleep pattern as soon as possible.

SLEEP ROUTINES

A good sleep routine isn't just for babies! A pre-bed routine can condition you for sleep. By repeating the same process every evening, your body will start to recognise that it's time for bed, helping you to feel relaxed and get off to sleep more easily. You might want to enjoy a warm drink, relax in a bath, lower the lights, listen to calming music, do a little meditation or read a book, all of which will help lift your mood as well as get you ready for bed.

> " If you're sleep-deprived, you're less likely to be able to make decisions, focus on tasks or enjoy activities "

HOW FOOD AFFECTS YOUR MOOD

What you eat can have a huge impact on your mood, so tweaking your diet could help improve your mental wellbeing

✦

Our day-to-day diet influences the way we feel, just as much as it impacts on our physical health. Certain foods are known to give us energy and improve our mood, just as other foods can negatively affect our mood.

It's best to choose foods that release energy slowly. Unfortunately, some of the tastiest foods, such as biscuits, chocolate and cakes, cause our blood sugar to rise rapidly and then fall just as quickly. This can lead to an energy slump, which in turn makes us feel low and tired. Instead, opt for foods like wholegrains (pasta, bread, rice), nuts or seeds, which keep your sugar levels balanced and your mood on an even keel.

EAT REGULARLY

Big meals can leave you feeling sluggish and groggy, so try to eat smaller meals at regular intervals to regulate your moods throughout the day. Don't skip meals – feeling hungry will also impact on your mood.

> **Keeping your sugar levels balanced will keep your mood on an even keel**

It's also important to eat good fats, which are essential to brain function. This includes things like olive oil, avocados, full-fat dairy products, oily fish and eggs. These foods will help with a positive mood, whereas the trans fats found in processed foods will have the opposite effect.

Plenty of fruits and vegetables are also essential to a positive mood – aim for at least your five a day, and try to eat a variety of colours each week to maximise the benefits. Protein is another key component, which can be found in lean meats, dairy products, legumes (e.g. beans, peas and lentils) and soya-based items.

What you drink will also impact on your mood. Caffeine can give you a little boost, but too much can leave you feeling low, anxious and depressed, as well as impacting on your sleep. Alcohol might make you feel good in the short term, but it will cause a blood sugar spike – not to mention how much overindulgence can impact your mood the day after. Staying hydrated and drinking plenty of water is important, as this will give you energy, focus and a positive mindset.

While it's always best to focus on wholefoods, you might wish to try vitamins or supplements to balance your moods. A good-quality multivitamin ensures you're getting everything your body needs each day. If you don't get enough good fats in your diet, consider an Omega-3 supplement. A vitamin B-complex might also help to lift your mood, as well as improve your energy levels and metabolism.

GUT HEALTH

Recent studies have shown a strong link between gut health and our moods. When you feel stressed or worried, do you get that tight feeling in the pit of your stomach? Our emotions and gut are intrinsically linked. Your gut is home to trillions of bacteria in a unique combination that makes up your own personal microbiome. If your microbiome is out of balance, this can contribute to stress, anxiety and low mood. Therefore, try to include gut-friendly food in your diet such as live yogurt, probiotic drinks or supplements, fruits and vegetables, wholegrains and pulses.

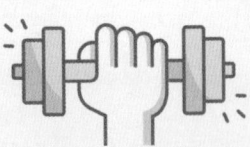

WHY PHYSICAL HEALTH MATTERS

Your physical health affects your mood and mental health, so incorporating some exercise into your day can give you a boost

Looking after your physical health can have a big impact on your mood. When you're feeling fit and well, you're likely to feel happier and more balanced too. You've probably noticed that when you're unwell, you feel sad and low – your body and mind are intrinsically linked.

Some aspects of our physical health are outside of our control, so it's important to focus on what you can do and not what you can't. Exercise is a key factor in our physical health and there are so many different ways of incorporating this into your life that there's sure to be something that suits you. If you find an exercise you enjoy, not only will you improve your physical health, but you'll get a mental health boost too.

LISTEN TO YOUR BODY

Overexercising can impact on your mood too, making you feel tired and run-down. Listen to what your body is telling you and take a rest day when you need to.

> **PHYSICAL HEALTH GOALS**
>
> Improving your physical health through exercise can take time. Break down what you want to achieve into smaller, more manageable goals – as you reach each goal, this will give you a little boost and the incentive to continue. Setting and meeting goals will also improve your mood. So, if you want to run 5km for example, then consider taking part in a Couch to 5K programme to guide you through step by step. Or maybe you want to set a target to walk more often and aim for three times a week around the block – over time you can make your walks more frequent and/or longer.

> "When we exercise, the brain releases endorphins, which make us feel happy, calm and energetic. Exercise also briefly distracts us from anything else that might be going on in our lives"

When we exercise, the brain releases endorphins, which make us feel happy, calm and energetic. Not only that, exercise distracts us from anything else that might be going on in our lives for a little bit, which can again help lift our mood. Exercise can help to relieve the symptoms of depression, anxiety and stress, so it's worth making it a habit. If you exercise regularly, you're more likely to maintain a healthy weight, and this in itself can help with your mood.

Illness or poor physical health can have a negative impact on mood. Serious, long-term, chronic conditions can cause a low mood and feelings of frustration. In these cases, it's worth speaking to your medical team about what exercise you can safely undertake and the benefits of this.

If you're unwell or injured in the short term, you may have to step down from your usual exercise routine while you recover. You might find that your mood drops if you're used to being more active. This can be hard to deal with, but it is important to take the time to recover properly so you can get back to doing what you love as soon as possible.

WHY MENTAL HEALTH MATTERS

Looking after your mental health is important when it comes to managing your moods, but a low mood can be the first sign of something wrong

Looking after your mental health is just as important as your physical health. Your mood day to day can be a sign of your mental health – one of the key symptoms of many mental health disorders is a persistent low mood.

Many of us will experience a mental health issue in our lifetime. One of the most common is stress. Stress is a natural reaction to feeling under pressure or threat, and we will all experience it from time to time. However, too much stress over a long period of time can affect our mood, leaving us feeling tired, irritable and anxious. Stress can also cause physical symptoms, such as headaches, tension, aches and pains, and poor gut health.

SELF-CARE

If you recognise that you're struggling with your mental health and low mood, take some time out to do something that you find enjoyable or relaxing. Self-care is important and should be regularly scheduled into your week.

We all suffer from a low mood sometimes, often triggered by events in our lives. However, sometimes these low moods happen for no reason. If you find that you're feeling low for a long period of time and don't feel like you're enjoying your usual activities, you may be experiencing depression.

Another common mental health problem is anxiety. Like stress, feeling anxious is a normal reaction to certain situations – such as taking a test, going to an interview, worrying about a loved one – but more severe anxiety can have a huge impact on daily life and is a long-term condition. Feeling anxious all the time has a knock-on effect on your mood, as you might find it hard to relax or enjoy activities.

If you recognise any of the signs of a mental health issue, you should seek help from a professional. There are plenty of options, from talking therapies to medication. There are some things you can do to help yourself – talking to someone you trust, engaging in some exercise, spending time outside, getting more sleep – but it's always best to have a chat with a doctor as well.

There are some more serious mental health disorders too, and it is important that these are diagnosed properly so that the right help and support can be sought.

MINDFULNESS & MEDITATION

Both mindfulness and meditation can help improve your mood. Mindfulness helps you to acknowledge your thoughts and feelings, and learn to pay attention to your present moment. You can practise mindfulness through your daily activities, such as on a walk or when cooking; by focusing on the task at hand and noticing what's around you with all your senses, you can feel more relaxed and calm. You can also try guided meditation practices at home, learning to focus on your breath and switch off from the outside world. These techniques are great for your mental health and can also boost your mood.

> **❝** Too much stress over a long period of time can affect our mood, leaving us feeling tired, irritable and anxious **❞**

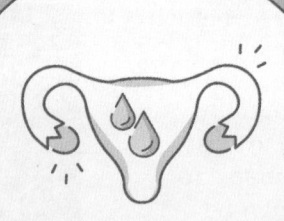

MENSTRUAL HEALTH AND MOODS

Your menstrual cycle can cause your moods to fluctuate during the month as your hormone levels rise and fall

✦

Your menstrual cycle can have a great impact on your moods, and you might find that your mood ebbs and flows throughout each month. The menstrual cycle is complex and there is a lot going on inside our bodies, so it's no wonder that this can affect the way we feel.

You have probably heard of PMS – premenstrual syndrome – which can occur in the weeks leading up to your period. Most women experience it to some extent, but for some it can have a greater effect on daily life than others. It's thought that PMS is triggered by a change in hormone levels during the menstrual cycle, and one of the most common symptoms is mood swings.

TRACK YOUR CYCLES

There is space in this journal to track your cycle and symptoms, along with your mood. By doing this every month, you should see a pattern emerge to help you prepare for future cycles.

> **Regular exercise and a balanced diet will help ease the rollercoaster of emotions, as will avoiding caffeine, alcohol and heavily processed foods**

At the start of a new menstrual cycle, i.e. the first day of your period, the hormones oestrogen and progesterone are low. Some studies have shown that low levels of these hormones can be linked to low levels of serotonin, which might explain a drop in mood around this time too. Not to mention that the physical symptoms of having a period – heavy bleeding, breast tenderness, cramps, pain, bloating – can also affect your mood.

Once your period has finished, your oestrogen and progesterone levels rise ready for ovulation. For some people, this boost in hormone levels can help your mood lift, but if you are sensitive to oestrogen, this change can leave you feeling anxious or on edge.

In short, your mood is likely to change throughout your own personal menstrual cycle. There are some things you can do to help ease the rollercoaster of emotions. Regular exercise and a balanced diet will help, as will avoiding caffeine, alcohol and heavily processed foods. There are some supplements that may help with the effects of hormonal changes too, such as probiotics (good gut health can help ease symptoms), vitamin E and vitamin B6, magnesium and calcium supplements. You can also get special blends that use a combination of herbal treatments to help balance your moods throughout your cycle.

MENOPAUSE

A natural part of ageing, the menopause is something that happens over a number of years when periods come to an end. It usually happens between 45 and 55 years old, but it can take many years of infrequent periods leading up to full menopause (the perimenopausal period). During perimenopause and menopause, oestrogen levels start to drop, causing symptoms, which can vary in severity. The most common symptoms are hot flushes, night sweats and a low mood. Being mindful of your diet and exercise can help lift your mood during this time, though there are options for hormone replacement or talking therapy.

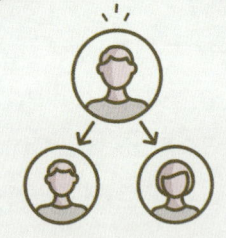

BALANCE YOUR SOCIAL LIFE

Your social life is important to your mood. Here are some tips for balancing your social life for the maximum benefits

Your social life is defined as 'the activities you do with other people, for pleasure, when you are not working'. It's important to have a social life, but what's right for one person won't be right for another. Some of us feel energised by spending lots of time with others, whereas some of us may feel drained, even if it's doing something we enjoy.

This is why finding a balance in your social life is key. Spending too much time on your own, not seeing others, can make you feel lonely and disconnected. Loneliness is known to impact on your mental health and contribute to a low mood. Anyone can feel lonely at any time. This might be especially true if, for example, you are working from

DIARISE YOUR SOCIAL LIFE

Plan your social activities and downtime into your diary just the same as you would work or health appointments. This can help to ensure the right balance for you.

INTROVERTS & EXTROVERTS

Your personality can have an impact on your social health, and understanding your needs will help you find a balance. Introverts generally prefer time alone, seeing one or two people at a time as opposed to larger groups, and need time alone after socialising to recharge. If you do too much or see too many people you might find that this negatively impacts your mood, so make sure you have plenty of downtime planned into your week. Extroverts tend to prefer to be with other people, rather than alone, and like bigger gatherings and meeting lots of new people. Being alone too much might cause a low mood, whereas being around other people can energise you, so make sure you plan in some fun activities throughout your week.

> **If there is no space in your calendar for downtime, you could suffer from social burnout**

home and you are missing out on the usual social conversations that happen in an office. Other life changes can trigger periods of loneliness too, such as retirement, changing jobs or becoming a parent.

It's important to recognise these feelings of loneliness. There are ways to regain a social life, but it can feel overwhelming at first. It's a great idea to start by thinking about hobbies you enjoy. You can then find groups and activities related to those where you will be able to meet like-minded people. There are groups aimed at new parents, at those who want to try a new sport for the first time, or networking events for those in the same profession to meet up and share ideas.

On the flipside, it's also possible to have too much of a social life. If you feel like you're always doing something and there is never any space in your calendar for downtime, you could suffer social burnout or social fatigue. We all have our own social limit and it's important to recognise when you're feeling like it's all too much. Low mood, low energy, irritability and trouble sleeping could all be signs of poor social health. Make sure you mark out some time in your diary when you're unavailable for socialising and use this time to relax, rest and recuperate.

WEATHER AND MOODS

Have you noticed that the weather can impact your mood, both positively and negatively? We have some advice for managing your mood seasonally

✦ ✳ ✦

There are a lot of external elements that can influence our moods that we have no control over, and one of these is the weather. On warm, sunny days you might find yourself uplifted and full of energy, whereas on gloomy, rainy days, you may feel sad or tired. Part of this is down to light exposure – during the summer months, we're exposed to more hours of light, whereas in winter, we have less light, which can make us feel more lethargic.

We're not a species that hibernates throughout the winter, but that doesn't mean our bodies don't feel the change of the seasons. It's instinctual on bad weather days to find shelter and warmth, and stay indoors

PLAN AHEAD

If you know a spell of bad weather is coming up, plan some fun indoor activities to look forward to so you don't feel you're missing out on doing anything just because of the weather.

a lot more. However, it is still important to expose yourself to light during the day – it's key to our circadian rhythm and can help us feel more balanced. A brisk walk in the wind and rain might be a little bracing, but it can help your mood too. If you can't face going outside in bad weather, try to sit near a window and let in as much light as possible for a drier mood boost.

Your mindset towards the weather can also influence your mood. If you focus on what you can't do due to weather conditions, you may find yourself feeling sad and low. You might feel that you're stuck at home and missing out on things you usually enjoy – this can be because it's too hot or too cold. If your mood is low, try to find some activities you enjoy that are not weather-dependent. On a really cold day, it can be wonderful to curl up with a favourite book and a hot drink under a blanket. If it's scorching hot outside, there is a lot of pleasure to be had from a dip in the cold sea or even a cold shower – it's invigorating and can lift your mood too.

SEASONAL AFFECTIVE DISORDER

Seasonal Affective Disorder (SAD) is a type of depression that occurs in a pattern with the seasons, and for some people it can really impact on their quality of life at certain times of the year. The symptoms are usually more apparent in winter, and include a persistent low mood, loss of interest in usual activities and lethargy, among others. It's thought that SAD could be caused by reduced exposure to daylight in the winter months, disrupting the body clock and the production of essential hormones. Treatment ranges from increased light exposure and exercise to therapy and medication.

> " A brisk walk in the wind and rain is bracing, but if you can't face going outside, sit near a window and let in as much light as possible "

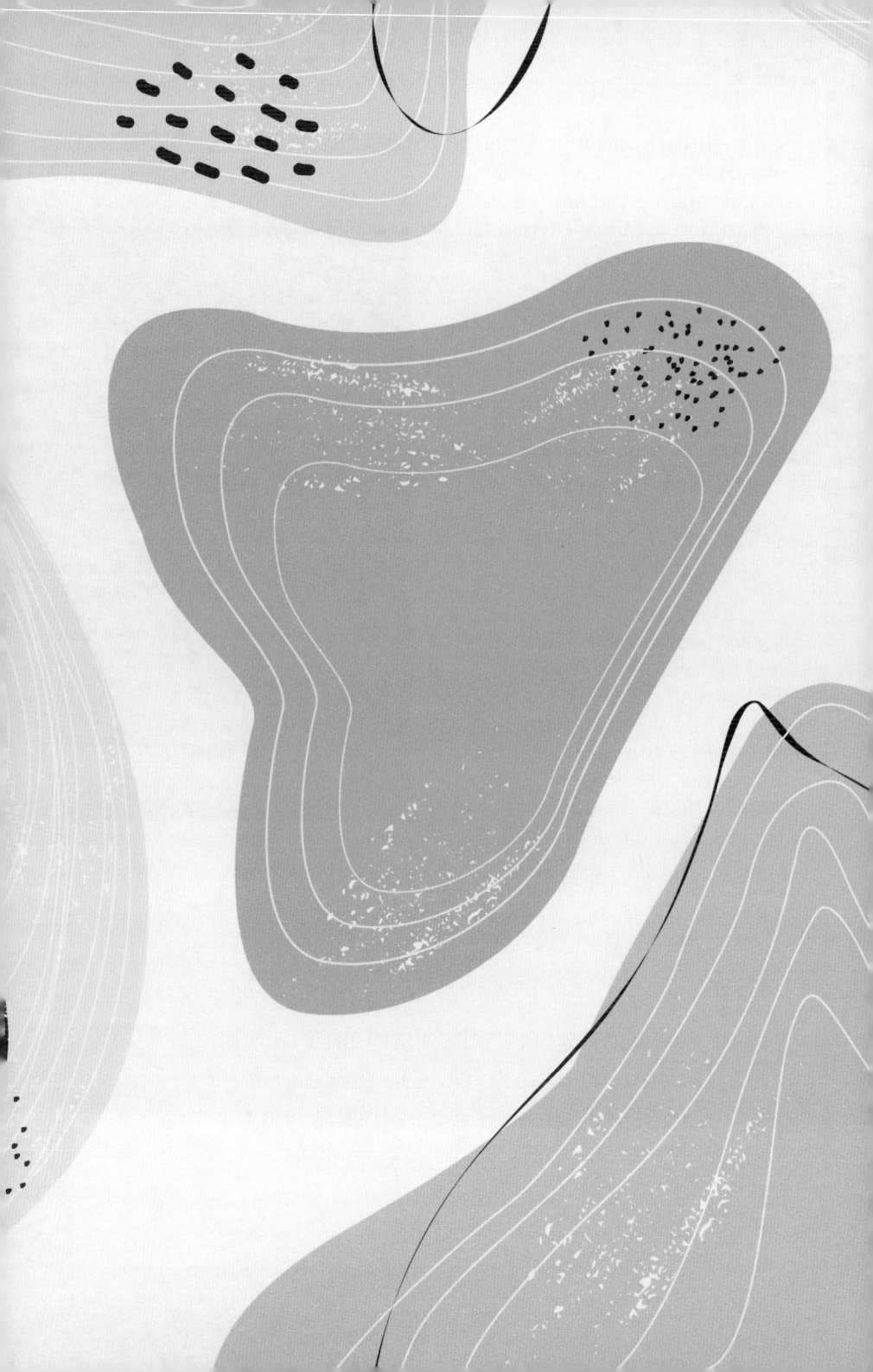

JOURNAL

26
MONTH ONE

40
MONTH TWO

54
MONTH THREE

68
MONTH FOUR

82
MONTH FIVE

96
MONTH SIX

110
MONTH SEVEN

124
MONTH EIGHT

138
MONTH NINE

152
MONTH TEN

166
MONTH ELEVEN

180
MONTH TWELVE

MONTHLY OVERVIEW

MONTH ONE

• Month _____   • Year _____

Notes

_____
_____
_____
_____
_____
_____
_____
_____
_____
_____
_____
_____

1	2	3	4	5	6	7
W.........	W.........	W.........	W.........	W.........	W.........	W.........
E.........	E.........	E.........	E.........	E.........	E.........	E.........
S.........	S.........	S.........	S.........	S.........	S.........	S.........

8	9	10	11	12	13	14
W.........	W.........	W.........	W.........	W.........	W.........	W.........
E.........	E.........	E.........	E.........	E.........	E.........	E.........
S.........	S.........	S.........	S.........	S.........	S.........	S.........

15	16	17	18	19	20	21
W.........	W.........	W.........	W.........	W.........	W.........	W.........
E.........	E.........	E.........	E.........	E.........	E.........	E.........
S.........	S.........	S.........	S.........	S.........	S.........	S.........

22	23	24	25	26	27	28
W.........	W.........	W.........	W.........	W.........	W.........	W.........
E.........	E.........	E.........	E.........	E.........	E.........	E.........
S.........	S.........	S.........	S.........	S.........	S.........	S.........

29	30	31				
W.........	W.........	W.........	Shade in each day and feel free to use more than one colour for each day!			
E.........	E.........	E.........				
S.........	S.........	S.........				

KEY

W - WEATHER
E - EXERCISE
S - SOCIAL

Sleep

Shade in the squares for each night and use the space below to record any relevant notes

_____

_____

_____

_____

_____

_____

_____

_____

_____

_____

_____

_____

MONTH ONE

HOURS ⟶

DATE	1	2	3	4	5	6	7	8	9+
1									
2									
3									
4									
5									
6									
7									
8									
9									
10									
11									
12									
13									
14									
15									
16									
17									
18									
19									
20									
21									
22									
23									
24									
25									
26									
27									
28									
29									
30									
31									

CHANGE YOUR SLEEP PATTERNS

Making tweaks to improve your sleep can make a big difference to your moods, but long-term changes won't happen overnight

SMALL ADJUSTMENTS

If you're trying to adapt how long you sleep, it's best to do it incrementally. If you want to start going to bed or getting up earlier than you do currently, change your current time a little each day and each week until you reach your target sleep window. This makes you more likely to fall into the new pattern than if you try to do it all in one go.

SLEEP TECH

While you want to shy away from most tech at bedtime, sleep tech can help you understand your sleep patterns a little better. Many smartwatches have sleep functions built in and there are specific sleep monitors you can buy too. These monitor both how long you sleep for and how deeply. Accuracy varies, but they can give you a handy guide.

DON'T WORRY

If you're trying to change your sleep to improve your moods, don't worry if you have one or two bad nights in the process where things don't go to plan. It's important not to dwell on it, as this might prevent you from sleeping well the following night. Just get back into your new routine as soon as possible – it's all part of the process of change.

Diet & Nutrition

Tick the squares for each day of the month. At the end of the month, look at this page alongside the 'Monthly Overview' to see if you spot any patterns

DATE ↓

	BREAKFAST	LUNCH	DINNER	2X HEALTHY SNACKS	VEGETABLES	FRUIT	GOOD FATS	PROTEIN	WHOLEGRAINS	AT LEAST 2 LITRES OF WATER	UNHEALTHY SNACKS	MORE THAN 4 CAFFEINATED DRINKS	ALCOHOL	VITAMINS/SUPPLEMENTS
1														
2														
3														
4														
5														
6														
7														
8														
9														
10														
11														
12														
13														
14														
15														
16														
17														
18														
19														
20														
21														
22														
23														
24														
25														
26														
27														
28														
29														
30														
31														

MONTH ONE

SIMPLE DIETARY CHANGES

Even making a few easy changes to your diet and nutrition can have an impact on your moods. Here are some tips to help you get started

FOCUS ON FIVE-A-DAY
One of the quickest ways to boost your moods is by increasing the amount of fruit and vegetables you eat in a day. Try to eat at least your five portions a day, with at least three of these being vegetables. This could be as simple as adding a side salad to your main meal or having a smoothie for breakfast. Eat as many different coloured fruits and vegetables as you can.

UP YOUR FATS
Don't shy away from healthy fats! These are essential for brain health, which in turn helps your mood. Try to have at least one portion of oily fish each week. If you don't eat fish, include seeds and/or nuts in your meals – a good seed mix makes a lovely, crunchy salad topper.

WATCH YOUR DRINKS
What you drink matters as much as what you eat. Aim for at least six to eight glasses of water each day for the maximum energy benefits. Also try swapping some of your caffeinated drinks for herbal teas, especially in the afternoons so that caffeine doesn't disturb your sleep. Limit the amount of alcohol you drink too.

PLANT FORWARD
You don't have to go vegetarian or vegan to boost your moods if you don't want to, but it is a good idea to prioritise plant-based foods that are great for lifting your mood. Think lots of fruits and vegetables, wholegrains, beans and legumes, seeds and nuts.

Physical Health

You can use words or emoji-style pictures to fill this bit in!

Keep track of your fitness for the month...

DATE	EXERCISE	HOW I FELT BEFORE, DURING AND AFTERWARDS

◊ How has your general physical health been this month? Any illnesses, injuries or aches and pains worth noting?

_____
_____
_____

MONTH ONE

INCREASE EXERCISE LEVELS

One way to improve your physical health and ultimately your mood is to introduce a little more activity into your life

START SMALL
Whether you do no exercise at all currently, or you're already active but want to add in something different (for example, strength work, yoga or cardio), the best thing to do is to increase incrementally. Even ten minutes a day adds up to a lot over the course of a week.

FOLLOW A PROGRAMME
There are some great online training programmes that you can follow to help you meet a specific goal. Maybe you want to try a Couch to 5K plan to get into running, or you could follow a strength-building plan that builds up week on week. Having a firm plan can help to keep you motivated.

USE YOUR COMMUTES
We're all so busy that sometimes it can feel difficult to fit physical activity into your day. If you can, why not adapt your commute to work by walking there, cycling or even getting off public transport a stop or two earlier? Not only will this boost your physical ability, but it will also give you a mental uplift so you begin work in a good mood.

GET OTHERS INVOLVED
A great way to stay motivated is to get family or friends to join you in your goals. Arrange to meet a friend for a walk, for example, and you will tick off a few mood-boosting tricks – exercise, fresh air and socialising. It also gives you something to look forward to, which can also lift your mood.

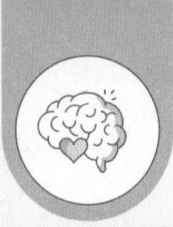

Mental Health

◇ Write down 5 things that have made you happy this month

_____
_____
_____
_____
_____

◇ Write down 5 things that have negatively impacted your mental health this month

_____
_____
_____
_____
_____

◇ What have you done to relax this month?

_____
_____

◇ What have you done to have fun this month?

_____
_____

MONTH ONE

MENTAL HEALTH AND MOOD

Your mood can be greatly affected by your mental health, so it's important to be aware of how to look after your mental wellbeing

PRIORITISE MENTAL HEALTH

Your mental health should be treated like your physical health. You need to be both physically and mentally fit to balance your moods, and a lot of the same techniques can help both. Exercise, self-care, good nutrition and plenty of sleep are key. And if you're feeling low, show yourself the same kindness you do when you're physically ill and take time to rest and recover.

LOW MOODS

It's normal to have low moods from time to time, even if you have good overall mental health. Tiredness, stress or worrying about something can all contribute to low moods. However, if you find your low moods last longer than usual or they are becoming more frequent, it's worth exploring your mental health.

POOR MENTAL HEALTH

Poor mental health and low mood are linked. If you are suffering emotionally, you might find it harder to do those things that bring you joy, which can in turn lead to a low mood, which can negatively affect your mental health further. It's a difficult cycle, but you can break it – we have some ideas throughout this section.

START SMALL

All of the sections in this journal work together. If you improve your sleep, nutrition, social contacts and physical health, these will all help your mental health too, and in turn boost your moods. However, trying to change everything at once can be overwhelming and this can negatively affect your mental health. Identify the areas you need to work on most and start small.

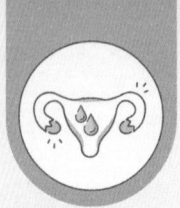

Menstrual Health

See page 7 on how to fill in the tracker

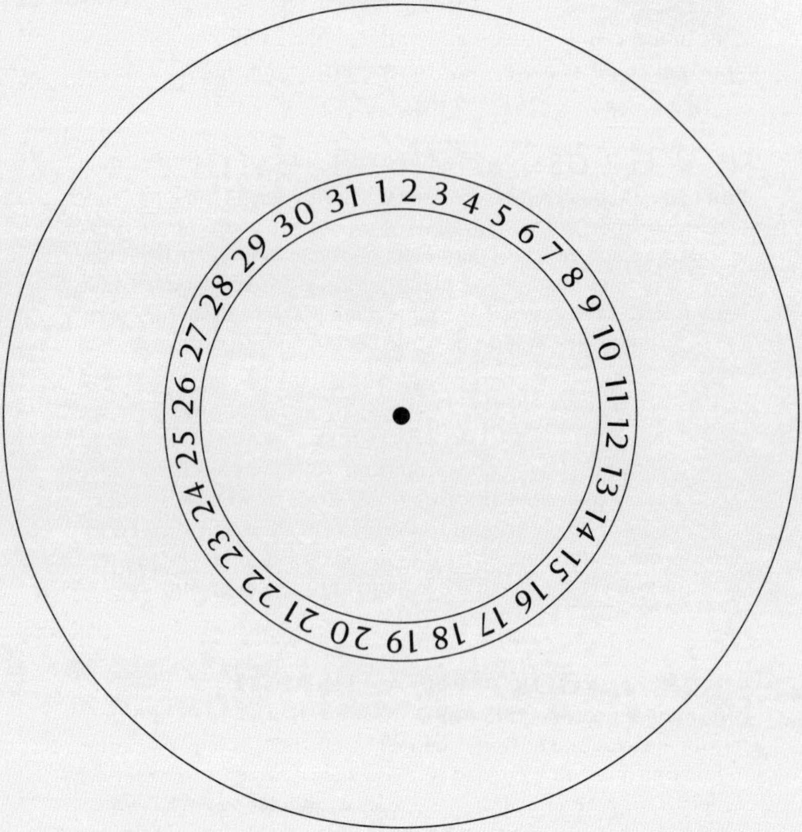

MONTH ONE

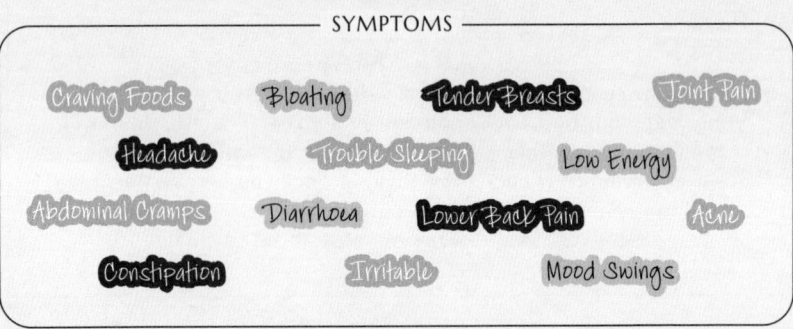

UNDERSTANDING PMS

Most women will suffer with some form of PMS, but what is it and why does it occur? Understanding what's happening in your body can help you to cope with it better

WHEN PMS OCCURS
Premenstrual syndrome (PMS) is a name for a group of symptoms (see below) that happen in the weeks leading up to your period. This happens in the luteal phase of your menstrual cycle, which is after ovulation. As this phase goes on, you might experience a drop in serotonin levels, which can impact your mood and emotions.

COMMON SYMPTOMS
Many women experience PMS symptoms around four to ten days before their period, and the severity of symptoms varies. The most common symptoms include mood swings, feeling upset or irritable, anxiety, trouble sleeping, fatigue, bloating, stomach pain, breast tenderness, headaches, skin problems and changes in appetite.

TRACK SYMPTOMS
Understanding your cycle and symptoms can help you to balance your moods throughout your cycle. When you know what to expect and when, you can prepare for the changes and put in place coping techniques. There is space throughout this journal to track your cycle and symptoms, so try to be consistent to see your patterns.

PMDD
Premenstrual dysphoric disorder (PMDD) is a severe form of PMS. While the symptoms are broadly the same, they are generally more intense and extreme. For example, headaches, muscle cramps or pains can prevent you doing normal activities. You may suffer from more intense emotional symptoms too, and become very anxious or depressed. It's important to talk to a doctor if you suspect PMDD.

Sociability

◇ Who have you seen this month outside of your household and workplace? Make a note of how these interactions made you feel

PERSON	WHEN/WHERE	HOW IT MADE YOU FEEL

◇ Make a note of any days you've felt lonely

_____

_____

◇ Has anyone been demanding of your time this month? Make a note of how it made you feel

_____

_____

MONTH ONE

THE IMPORTANCE OF BEING SOCIAL

We are born into a social group and live our lives as part of a society. Humans are naturally social creatures, and this can affect our moods

SHARED EXPERIENCES

No matter what it is you enjoy in life – exercise, hobbies, entertainment and so on – sharing your passions with others can enhance the experience. It gives mutual topics of conversation, and helps you to meet and bond with like-minded people, in turn boosting your mood and making you feel more content.

BALANCE IT

It's important to find a good balance in your social life, with enough social contact and enough alone time to keep you feeling good. This balance will be different for everyone, so don't worry if you need to be around people more than others, or if you crave lots of time by yourself.

FACE TO FACE

Where possible, social interactions are best in person. We have a plethora of tools to help us connect with people digitally, but to get the biggest mood benefits, it's better to meet up face to face. Seeing a friend can increase oxytocin (feel happy), lower cortisol (less stress) and produce dopamine (feel pleasure).

SUPPORT FROM FRIENDS

It's been shown that when we're going through tough times, we cope better when we feel supported by friends and family. Sometimes social contact isn't just about having fun and sharing experiences, it's about having someone trusted to talk to and be comforted by.

MONTHLY OVERVIEW

MONTH TWO

• Month _____   • Year _____

Notes

1	2	3	4	5	6	7
W........	W........	W........	W........	W........	W........	W........
E........	E........	E........	E........	E........	E........	E........
S........	S........	S........	S........	S........	S........	S........
8	9	10	11	12	13	14
W........	W........	W........	W........	W........	W........	W........
E........	E........	E........	E........	E........	E........	E........
S........	S........	S........	S........	S........	S........	S........
15	16	17	18	19	20	21
W........	W........	W........	W........	W........	W........	W........
E........	E........	E........	E........	E........	E........	E........
S........	S........	S........	S........	S........	S........	S........
22	23	24	25	26	27	28
W........	W........	W........	W........	W........	W........	W........
E........	E........	E........	E........	E........	E........	E........
S........	S........	S........	S........	S........	S........	S........
29	30	31	Shade in each day and feel free to use more than one colour for each day!			
W........	W........	W........				
E........	E........	E........				
S........	S........	S........				

KEY
W - WEATHER
E - EXERCISE
S - SOCIAL

Sleep

Shade in the squares for each night and use the space below to record any relevant notes

HOURS →

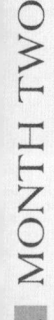

1 2 3 4 5 6 7 8 9+

DATE ↓

1–31

MONTH TWO

SLEEP AUDIT

Use this page to look at your current sleep patterns and how they might be affecting your moods. This should help you to identify whether you are getting a good quality of sleep

✶

Answer the questions below honestly to build up a picture of your current sleep quality.

How long, on average, does it take you to fall asleep at night?

_____

Do you sleep through the night, or do you wake up often? If you wake up often, how many times?

_____

Do you have a good bedtime routine?

_____

Do you often wake up feeling tired, grumpy or sad?

_____

Do you feel tired during the day? How does this affect your mood?

_____

Finally, on a scale from 1 (poor) to 5 (great), how would you rate your current sleep quality?

1   2   3   4   5

Diet & Nutrition

Tick the squares for each day of the month. At the end of the month, look at this page alongside the 'Monthly Overview' to see if you spot any patterns

DATE ↓

	BREAKFAST	LUNCH	DINNER	2X HEALTHY SNACKS	VEGETABLES	FRUIT	GOOD FATS	PROTEIN	WHOLEGRAINS	AT LEAST 2 LITRES OF WATER	UNHEALTHY SNACKS	MORE THAN 4 CAFFEINATED DRINKS	ALCOHOL	VITAMINS/SUPPLEMENTS
1														
2														
3														
4														
5														
6														
7														
8														
9														
10														
11														
12														
13														
14														
15														
16														
17														
18														
19														
20														
21														
22														
23														
24														
25														
26														
27														
28														
29														
30														
31														

MONTH TWO

YOUR NUTRITION GOALS

Use this page to think about what you'd like to achieve in your diet to help boost your moods. Setting clear goals can help you to stay motivated when making lifestyle changes

✳

What I would like to change about my current diet

_____

_____

_____

Foods I would like to include more of in my diet going forwards

_____

_____

_____

Foods I would like to eat less of going forwards

_____

_____

_____

How I hope making changes to my diet will affect my moods

_____

_____

_____

Physical Health

You can use words or emoji-style pictures to fill this bit in!

Keep track of your fitness for the month...

DATE	EXERCISE	HOW I FELT BEFORE, DURING AND AFTERWARDS		

◇ How has your general physical health been this month? Any illnesses, injuries or aches and pains worth noting?

_____
_____
_____

MONTH TWO

WHAT IS PHYSICAL HEALTH?

This page gives you a chance to think about what physical health means to you – it's different for all of us. This can help you to decide what you need to work on

✳

What does physical health look like to you? Is it the ability to do a certain sport or feel a certain way? Do you think you need to lose or gain weight to feel healthier? Is it about improving your stamina or your strength? Use this space to write down what you think is good physical health.

_____
_____
_____
_____
_____

What obstacles do you think are standing in your way towards achieving the physical health you desire?

_____
_____
_____
_____
_____
_____

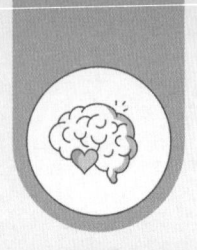

Mental Health

◇ Write down 5 things that have made you happy this month

_____
_____
_____
_____
_____

◇ Write down 5 things that have negatively impacted your mental health this month

_____
_____
_____
_____
_____

◇ What have you done to relax this month?

_____
_____

◇ What have you done to have fun this month?

_____
_____

YOUR CURRENT MENTAL HEALTH

You might not have given as much thought to your mental health as your physical health. This mini-audit can help you to identify any specific areas where you might have issues

✳

Answer the questions below honestly to build up
a picture of your current mental health.

Do you find it hard to focus on tasks and lack concentration?

___

Are you worrying about things more than usual?

___

Do you feel tired a lot of the time and lack energy?

___

Are you sleeping more or less than usual?

___

Are you avoiding your usual social activities?

___

Do you feel more emotional or tearful than usual?

___

Finally, on a scale from 1 (poor) to 5 (great), how would you rate your current mental health?

1   2   3   4   5

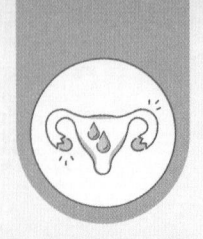

Menstrual Health

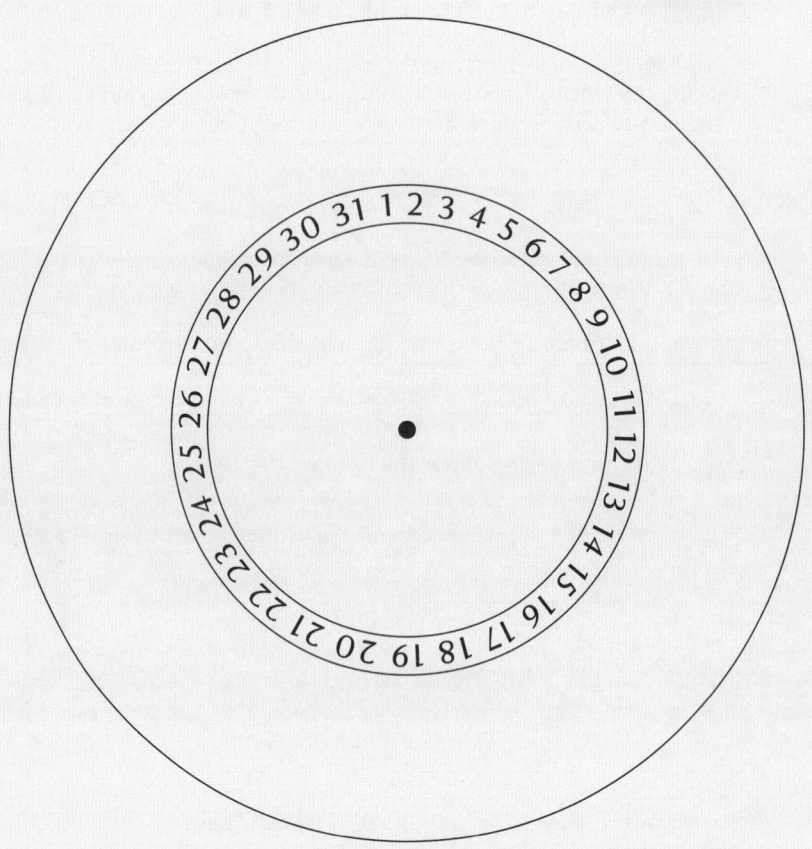

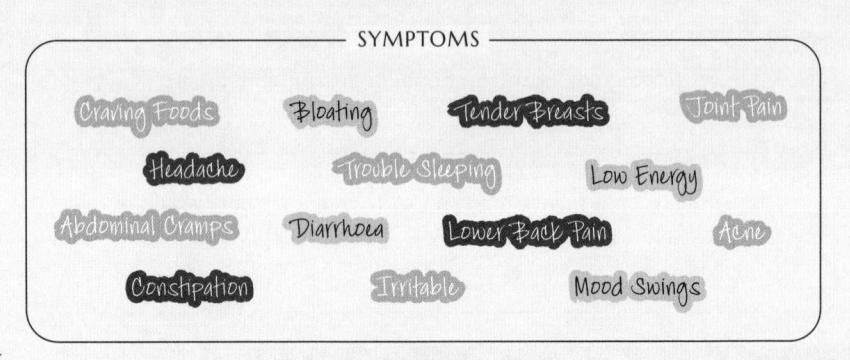

See page 7 on how to fill in the tracker

Days: 1 2 3 4 5 6 7 8 9 10 11 12 13 14 15 16 17 18 19 20 21 22 23 24 25 26 27 28 29 30 31

SYMPTOMS

- Craving Foods
- Bloating
- Tender Breasts
- Joint Pain
- Headache
- Trouble Sleeping
- Low Energy
- Abdominal Cramps
- Diarrhoea
- Lower Back Pain
- Acne
- Constipation
- Irritable
- Mood Swings

MONTH TWO

MANAGING YOUR PMS

Use this checklist to identify any areas that you
think could be contributing to your PMS symptoms.
This can help you make a plan for future cycles

✹

Do this activity on a day when you feel your PMS symptoms are
at their worst. Tick the boxes that apply to you; each of these
strategies can ease the severity of PMS symptoms.

TODAY'S DATE:
DATE NEXT PERIOD DUE:

	YES	NO
I have done some exercise today	☐	☐
I have eaten healthy, balanced meals	☐	☐
I have had seven to eight hours' sleep	☐	☐
I have had adequate opportunity to rest	☐	☐
I have done some stretching/yoga/Pilates	☐	☐
I have used some form of pain relief (painkillers, heat pad and so on)	☐	☐
I have had at least eight glasses of water	☐	☐

During your next cycle, try to do all of the above
strategies and see if your symptoms improve.

Sociability

◊ Who have you seen this month outside of your household and workplace? Make a note of how these interactions made you feel

PERSON	WHEN/WHERE	HOW IT MADE YOU FEEL

◊ Make a note of any days you've felt lonely

◊ Has anyone been demanding of your time this month? Make a note of how it made you feel

CURRENT SOCIAL HEALTH

Use this page to look at your current level of sociability. The prompts will help you to build up a picture of your social contact and time alone

✦

Answer the questions below honestly to build up a picture of your current social health.

How many days a week do you meet a friend/friends for a social activity?

___

Would you like to spend more time seeing others?

___

How often do you spend time on your own?

___

Would you like to have more time to yourself?

___

Would you describe yourself as an introvert, an extrovert, or somewhere in the middle?

___

Finally, on a scale from 1 (poor) to 5 (great), how would you rate the balance of your current social life?

1   2   3   4   5

MONTHLY OVERVIEW

MONTH THREE

- Month _____   - Year _____

Notes

1	2	3	4	5	6	7
W.........	W.........	W.........	W.........	W.........	W.........	W.........
E.........	E.........	E.........	E.........	E.........	E.........	E.........
S.........	S.........	S.........	S.........	S.........	S.........	S.........

8	9	10	11	12	13	14
W.........	W.........	W.........	W.........	W.........	W.........	W.........
E.........	E.........	E.........	E.........	E.........	E.........	E.........
S.........	S.........	S.........	S.........	S.........	S.........	S.........

15	16	17	18	19	20	21
W.........	W.........	W.........	W.........	W.........	W.........	W.........
E.........	E.........	E.........	E.........	E.........	E.........	E.........
S.........	S.........	S.........	S.........	S.........	S.........	S.........

22	23	24	25	26	27	28
W.........	W.........	W.........	W.........	W.........	W.........	W.........
E.........	E.........	E.........	E.........	E.........	E.........	E.........
S.........	S.........	S.........	S.........	S.........	S.........	S.........

29	30	31
W.........	W.........	W.........
E.........	E.........	E.........
S.........	S.........	S.........

KEY
W - WEATHER
E - EXERCISE
S - SOCIAL

Shade in each day and feel free to use more than one colour for each day!

Sleep

Shade in the squares for each night and use the space below to record any relevant notes

_____
_____
_____
_____
_____
_____
_____
_____
_____
_____
_____
_____
_____

MONTH THREE

HOURS ⟶

DATE	1	2	3	4	5	6	7	8	9+
1									
2									
3									
4									
5									
6									
7									
8									
9									
10									
11									
12									
13									
14									
15									
16									
17									
18									
19									
20									
21									
22									
23									
24									
25									
26									
27									
28									
29									
30									
31									

SETTING YOUR SLEEP GOALS

If you've identified some areas you'd like to work on in relation to your sleep, you can use the activities on this page to list your goals in more detail

✳

Use this space to list the specific things you wish to improve with regards to your sleep quality. The tips and activities in the rest of this journal will give you advice on how to make the changes you've identified

_____

_____

_____

_____

_____

_____

_____

_____

_____

_____

How many hours do you currently sleep, on average, per night? ____
How many hours would you like to set as your sleep goal going forward? ____

Diet & Nutrition

Tick the squares for each day of the month. At the end of the month, look at this page alongside the 'Monthly Overview' to see if you spot any patterns

MONTH THREE

DATE ↓

Date	BREAKFAST	LUNCH	DINNER	2X HEALTHY SNACKS	VEGETABLES	FRUIT	GOOD FATS	PROTEIN	WHOLEGRAINS	AT LEAST 2 LITRES OF WATER	UNHEALTHY SNACKS	MORE THAN 4 CAFFEINATED DRINKS	ALCOHOL	VITAMINS/SUPPLEMENTS
1														
2														
3														
4														
5														
6														
7														
8														
9														
10														
11														
12														
13														
14														
15														
16														
17														
18														
19														
20														
21														
22														
23														
24														
25														
26														
27														
28														
29														
30														
31														

FOOD FOR ENJOYMENT

Eating is as much about enjoyment as it is about being healthy. Foods can lift our moods by bringing comfort, triggering fond memories or being part of an overall experience

FOOD I ENJOY EATING	HOW IT MAKES ME FEEL
e.g. Tomato soup and bread	e.g. Warm and comforted on cold days

Write down a favourite food-related memory. Maybe you enjoyed cooking a certain meal with a relative or you had an amazing meal on holiday. Think about how it made you feel at the time

_____

_____

_____

How could you re-create that feeling now?

_____

_____

_____

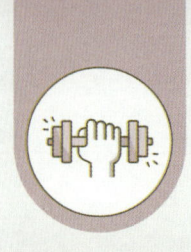

Physical Health

You can use words or emoji-style pictures to fill this bit in!

Keep track of your fitness for the month...

DATE	EXERCISE	HOW I FELT BEFORE, DURING AND AFTERWARDS

⋄ How has your general physical health been this month? Any illnesses, injuries or aches and pains worth noting?

_____
_____
_____

MONTH THREE

YOUR CURRENT PHYSICAL HEALTH

Here we explore your current physical health so you can see where you're at right now. This will help you to identify the areas you want to improve

✦

Answer the questions below honestly to build up a picture of your current physical health.

Do you exercise currently? If so, how often do you exercise?

_____

Do you often feel rundown or ill?

_____

Do you spend a lot of the day inactive (e.g. sitting down at a desk for work)?

_____

Do you often feel lethargic and lacking in energy?

_____

Do you think that there is room to improve your physical health?

_____

Finally, on a scale from 1 (poor) to 5 (great), how would you rate your current physical health?

1   2   3   4   5

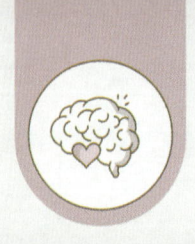

Mental Health

◇ Write down 5 things that have made you happy this month

_____
_____
_____
_____
_____

◇ Write down 5 things that have negatively impacted your mental health this month

_____
_____
_____
_____
_____

◇ What have you done to relax this month?

_____
_____

◇ What have you done to have fun this month?

_____
_____

MONTH THREE

MENTAL HEALTH INFLUENCES

Use the space on this page to think about what things affect your mental health. You might find that not getting outside enough is a negative influence, and exercise is a positive influence, for example, but this is personal to you

What things do you think negatively affect your mental health?

_____

_____

_____

_____

_____

What things do you think positively affect your mental health?

_____

_____

_____

_____

_____

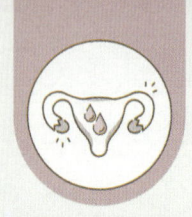

Menstrual Health

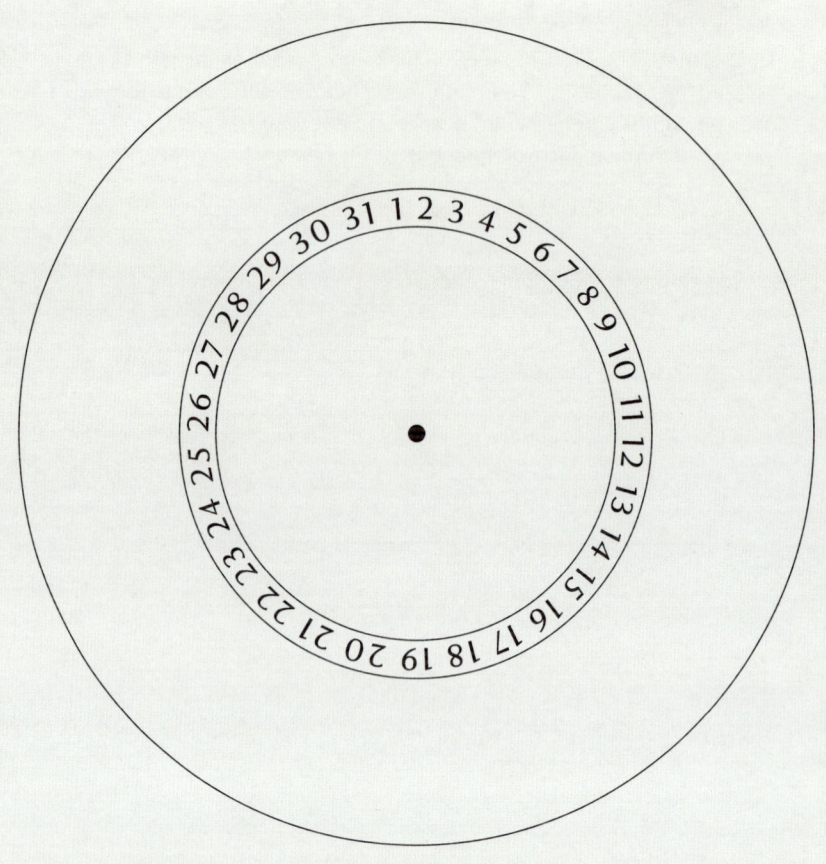

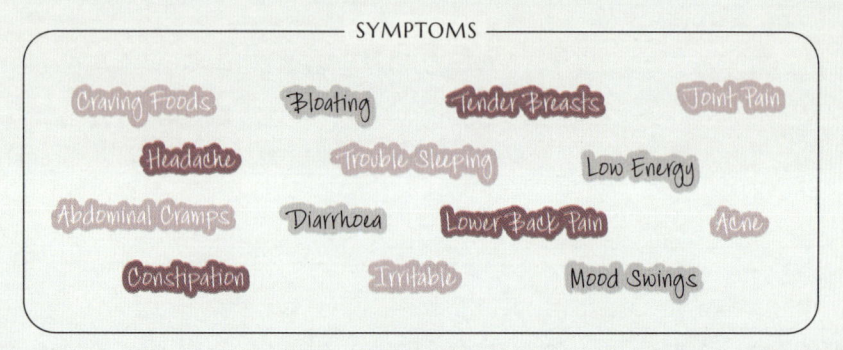

See page 7 on how to fill in the tracker

28 29 30 31 1 2 3 4 5 6 7 8 9 10 11 12 13 14 15 16 17 18 19 20 21 22 23 24 25 26 27

MONTH THREE

--- SYMPTOMS ---

Craving Foods • Bloating • Tender Breasts • Joint Pain
Headache • Trouble Sleeping • Low Energy
Abdominal Cramps • Diarrhoea • Lower Back Pain • Acne
Constipation • Irritable • Mood Swings

YOUR PMS PLAN

Every woman is different, so you will need your own plan for coping with PMS, depending on what you struggle with. Use this page to identify your problem areas and think about some solutions

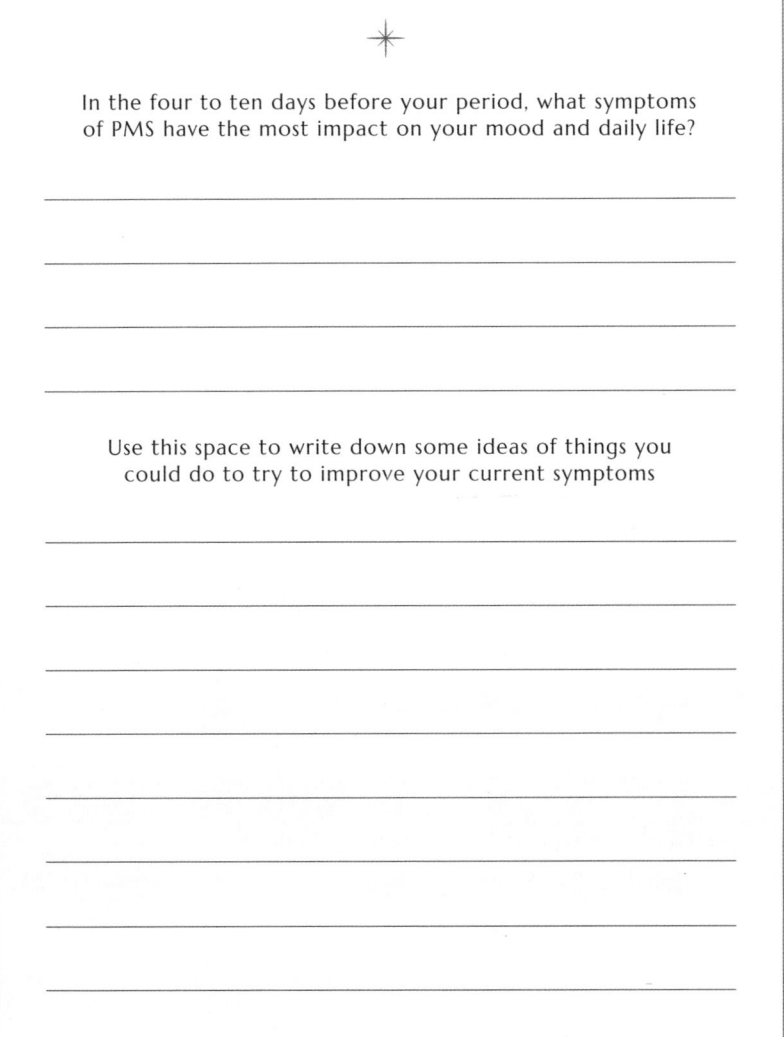

※

In the four to ten days before your period, what symptoms of PMS have the most impact on your mood and daily life?

_____

_____

_____

Use this space to write down some ideas of things you could do to try to improve your current symptoms

_____

_____

_____

_____

_____

_____

Sociability

◊ Who have you seen this month outside of your household and workplace? Make a note of how these interactions made you feel

PERSON	WHEN/WHERE	HOW IT MADE YOU FEEL

◊ Make a note of any days you've felt lonely

_____

_____

◊ Has anyone been demanding of your time this month? Make a note of how it made you feel

_____

_____

MONTH THREE

COMMIT TO CHANGE

If you feel like there are improvements you could make in your social life to help balance your moods, use this page to think about what you could change

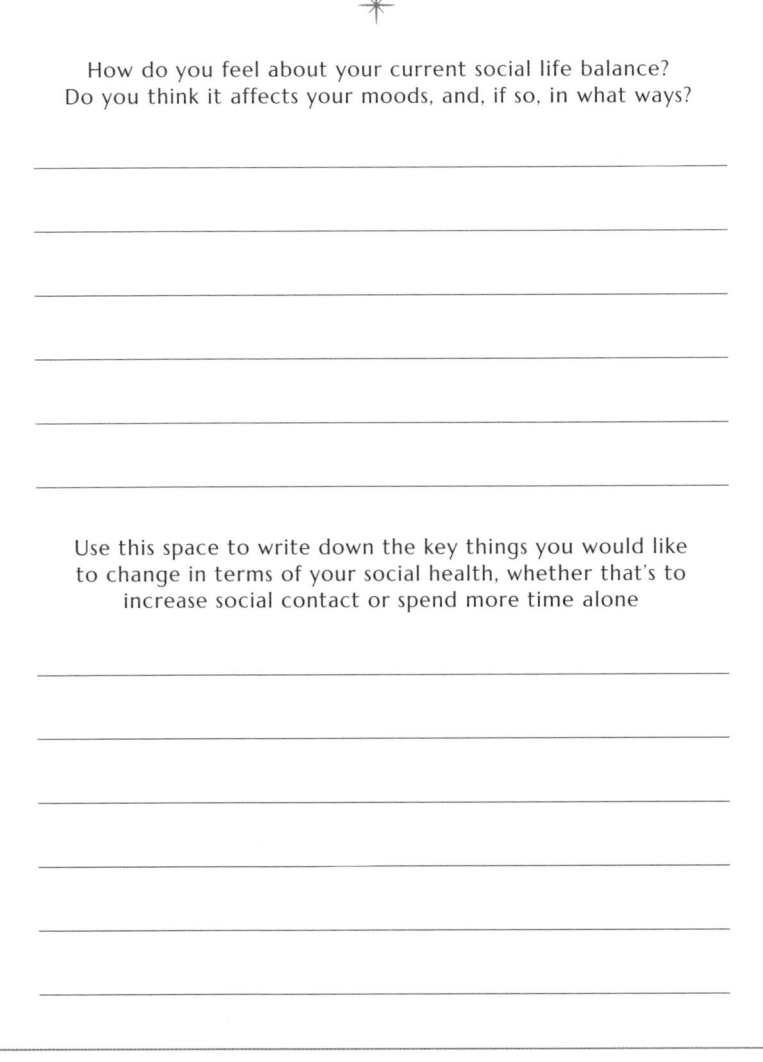

※

How do you feel about your current social life balance? Do you think it affects your moods, and, if so, in what ways?

_____

_____

_____

_____

_____

Use this space to write down the key things you would like to change in terms of your social health, whether that's to increase social contact or spend more time alone

_____

_____

_____

_____

_____

… MONTHLY OVERVIEW …

MONTH FOUR

• Month _____   • Year _____

Notes

1	2	3	4	5	6	7
W.........	W.........	W.........	W.........	W.........	W.........	W.........
E.........	E.........	E.........	E.........	E.........	E.........	E.........
S.........	S.........	S.........	S.........	S.........	S.........	S.........

8	9	10	11	12	13	14
W.........	W.........	W.........	W.........	W.........	W.........	W.........
E.........	E.........	E.........	E.........	E.........	E.........	E.........
S.........	S.........	S.........	S.........	S.........	S.........	S.........

15	16	17	18	19	20	21
W.........	W.........	W.........	W.........	W.........	W.........	W.........
E.........	E.........	E.........	E.........	E.........	E.........	E.........
S.........	S.........	S.........	S.........	S.........	S.........	S.........

22	23	24	25	26	27	28
W.........	W.........	W.........	W.........	W.........	W.........	W.........
E.........	E.........	E.........	E.........	E.........	E.........	E.........
S.........	S.........	S.........	S.........	S.........	S.........	S.........

29	30	31	Shade in each day and feel free to use more than one colour for each day!
W.........	W.........	W.........	
E.........	E.........	E.........	
S.........	S.........	S.........	

KEY

W - WEATHER
E - EXERCISE
S - SOCIAL

Sleep

Shade in the squares for each night and use the space below to record any relevant notes

HOURS →

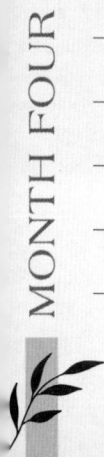

DATE

MONTH FOUR

IMPROVE YOUR SLEEP

If you want to boost your moods by sleeping deeply for longer, we have some tips and tricks to help you make the changes you need

TOTAL DARKNESS
Have you ever stopped to look at how dark your bedroom actually is? There could be light leaking in from outside sources, or there could be a glow from devices and clocks. Ideally you want to make your room as close to pitch black as possible to encourage deep sleep. If that's not possible, consider wearing a sleep mask instead.

LIMIT BED USE
Your bed should only be used for sleep and relationships – too many of us use our bed to do other things, such as scrolling through our phones, working on a laptop or watching TV. You want your brain to associate your bed with sleep, not all those other activities, so limit what you use it for.

REGULAR SCHEDULE
You should aim to always wake at the same time and go to bed at the same time where possible. This will help your body learn to be sleepy at the right time and ensure you wake full of energy the next day. The odd late night or lie-in won't matter too much, but try not to make it a habit.

LOWER THE LIGHTS
You can start preparing your brain for sleep by dimming the lights a couple of hours before bedtime. This will signal the brain that it's time to start relaxing, and by the time you get into bed, you'll be ready to drift off as quickly as possible.

Diet & Nutrition

Tick the squares for each day of the month. At the end of the month, look at this page alongside the 'Monthly Overview' to see if you spot any patterns

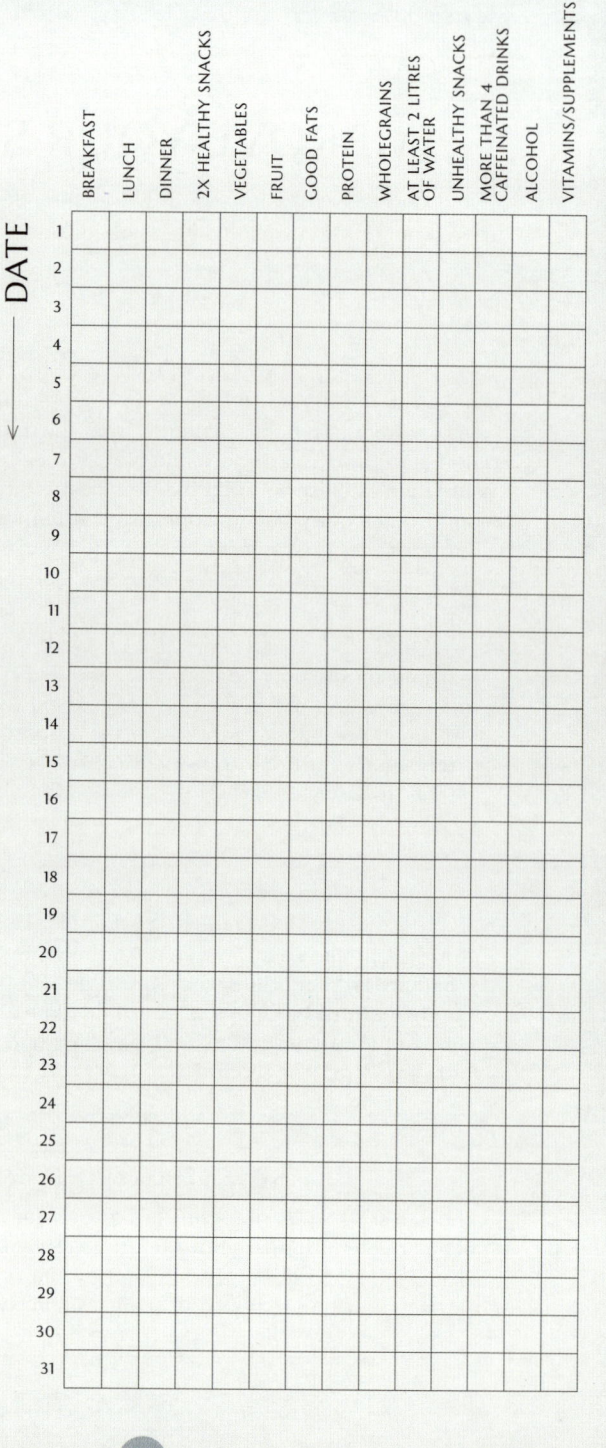

DATE →

	BREAKFAST	LUNCH	DINNER	2X HEALTHY SNACKS	VEGETABLES	FRUIT	GOOD FATS	PROTEIN	WHOLEGRAINS	AT LEAST 2 LITRES OF WATER	UNHEALTHY SNACKS	MORE THAN 4 CAFFEINATED DRINKS	ALCOHOL	VITAMINS/SUPPLEMENTS
1														
2														
3														
4														
5														
6														
7														
8														
9														
10														
11														
12														
13														
14														
15														
16														
17														
18														
19														
20														
21														
22														
23														
24														
25														
26														
27														
28														
29														
30														
31														

MONTH FOUR

MOOD-BOOSTING BREAKFASTS

Start your day the right way by making sure your breakfast is packed with mood-lifting ingredients to boost your energy and fill you up

START WITH OATS

Oats make a good base for a breakfast. They are good for slow-release energy throughout the day, which will help to balance your blood sugar and your moods. You could have porridge or overnight oats with a variety of toppings (such as nut butter, seeds or berries) to boost the benefits.

EGG BENEFITS

Eggs are a great breakfast option. They are a good source of protein and also contain vitamin D and vitamin B12. The yolks also contain choline, an essential nutrient that helps support the brain and nervous system, playing a role in regulating your moods.

Use this space to list five mood-boosting breakfast ideas that you can refer back to when you need some inspiration.

1. _____
2. _____
3. _____
4. _____
5. _____

Physical Health

You can use words or emoji-style pictures to fill this bit in!

Keep track of your fitness for the month...

DATE	EXERCISE	HOW I FELT BEFORE, DURING AND AFTERWARDS			

◇ How has your general physical health been this month? Any illnesses, injuries or aches and pains worth noting?

_____
_____
_____

MONTH FOUR

PHYSICAL HEALTH GOALS

Use the space on this page to set some goals that you can work towards to improve your physical health

✦

What are your main goals when it comes to improving your physical health?

_____

_____

_____

_____

_____

_____

What steps/mini-goals can you work towards to help achieve your main goals?

_____

_____

_____

_____

_____

_____

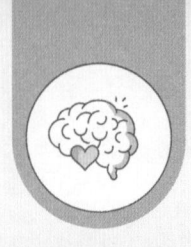

Mental Health

◇ Write down 5 things that have made you happy this month

_____

_____

_____

_____

_____

◇ Write down 5 things that have negatively impacted your mental health this month

_____

_____

_____

_____

_____

◇ What have you done to relax this month?

_____

_____

◇ What have you done to have fun this month?

_____

_____

MONTH FOUR

LEARN NEW SKILLS

Taking the time to learn something new can have a great impact on your mental health and your mood, but it doesn't have to be complicated

✧

CONFIDENCE BOOST

When we master something new, it helps to boost confidence and self-esteem, which in turn helps our mental health and our mood. It can be something as simple as a new recipe or finishing a puzzle, or something bigger like learning a new language. Set yourself a goal to try a new thing every month.

✧

SENSE OF PURPOSE

Feeling like you have a sense of purpose has a positive impact on your mental health and mood. This is why continuing learning and developing can have such a big impact – working towards and achieving a goal helps to give us that sense of purpose.

✧

Use this space to write down some new things you would love to try, big or small.

_____

_____

_____

_____

_____

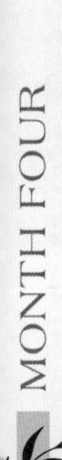

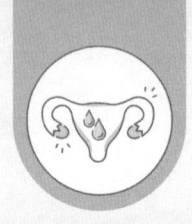

Menstrual Health

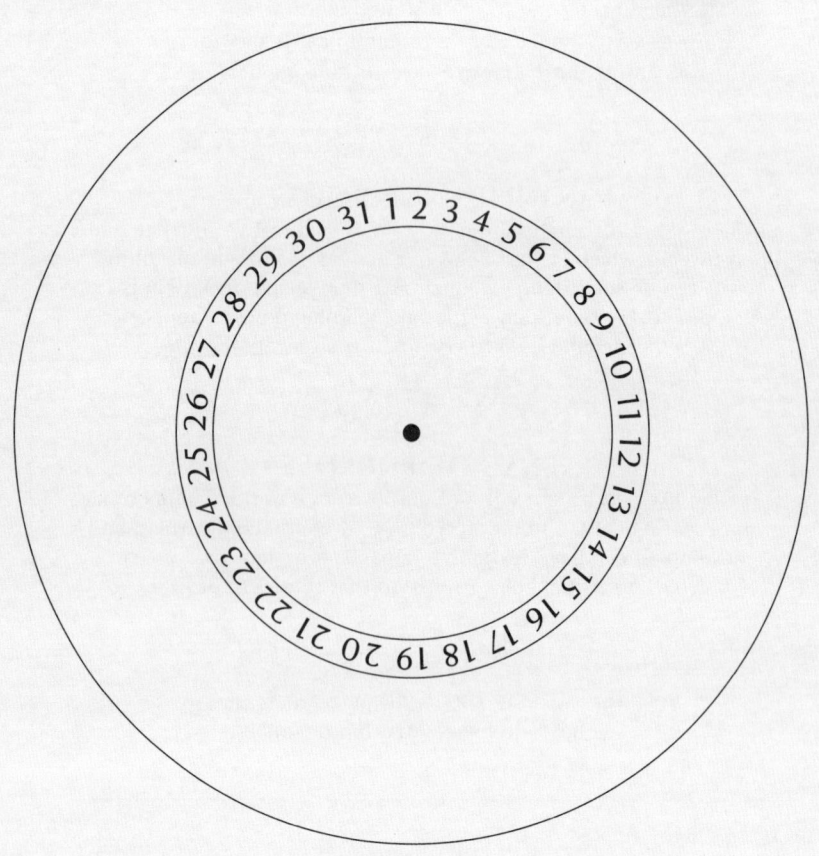

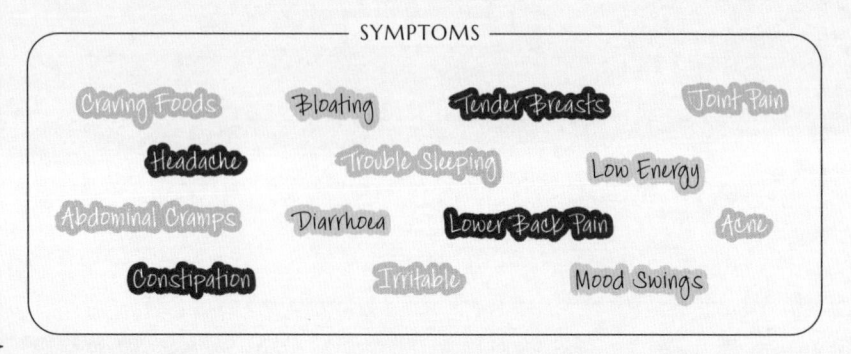

See page 7 on how to fill in the tracker

29 30 31 1 2 3 4 5 6 7 8 9 10 11 12 13 14 15 16 17 18 19 20 21 22 23 24 25 26 27 28

— SYMPTOMS —

- Craving Foods
- Bloating
- Tender Breasts
- Joint Pain
- Headache
- Trouble Sleeping
- Low Energy
- Abdominal Cramps
- Diarrhoea
- Lower Back Pain
- Acne
- Constipation
- Irritable
- Mood Swings

MONTH FOUR

EATING FOR PMS

Some foods have been shown to potentially improve PMS. It's worth taking a look at your diet in the two weeks before your period to see if you can make any changes

✦

PMS POWER FOODS

Here are some ideas of foods to try to incorporate into your diet in the luteal stage of your menstrual cycle (when PMS is most likely): eggs, calcium-rich foods such as yoghurt, oily fish such as salmon, cruciferous vegetables such as broccoli, and magnesium-rich foods such as pumpkin seeds, almonds, cashews and bananas.

✦

PMS SUPPLEMENTS

There are plenty of supplements out there that promote relief from PMS symptoms. While you are better trying for a healthy, balanced diet, there are some supplements that might help. You could try taking vitamin B6, calcium, vitamin D and magnesium, and see if these improve your symptoms.

✦

Use this space to write down a new meal or snack you'd like to try in your next cycle that incorporates some PMS-relieving foods.

_____

_____

_____

_____

_____

_____

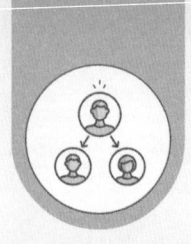

Sociability

◇ Who have you seen this month outside of your household and workplace? Make a note of how these interactions made you feel

PERSON	WHEN/WHERE	HOW IT MADE YOU FEEL

◇ Make a note of any days you've felt lonely

_____

_____

◇ Has anyone been demanding of your time this month? Make a note of how it made you feel

_____

_____

MONTH FOUR

SOCIAL MEDIA

A lot of modern socialising happens online, which can have its benefits, but can also affect our moods and mental health

POSITIVE SOCIAL MEDIA
Used the right way, social media can have a lot of benefits. It helps us to stay in contact with people over vast distances and from different times in our life. It can make us feel connected, even when we're alone. Take a bit of time to think about what positive benefits you get from social media, if you use it.

MONITOR USE
Social media shouldn't be used to replace physical social contact, so it's worth monitoring how much you use it. There are tools and apps for your phone and other devices that monitor your screen time, and it can be worth installing these if you think you're spending too much time online.

How many hours per day do you spend on social media, on average?

_____

Do you think this is too much or about right?

_____

_____

_____

MONTHLY OVERVIEW

MONTH FIVE

• Month _____ • Year _____

Notes

1	2	3	4	5	6	7
W.........	W.........	W.........	W.........	W.........	W.........	W.........
E.........	E.........	E.........	E.........	E.........	E.........	E.........
S.........	S.........	S.........	S.........	S.........	S.........	S.........

8	9	10	11	12	13	14
W.........	W.........	W.........	W.........	W.........	W.........	W.........
E.........	E.........	E.........	E.........	E.........	E.........	E.........
S.........	S.........	S.........	S.........	S.........	S.........	S.........

15	16	17	18	19	20	21
W.........	W.........	W.........	W.........	W.........	W.........	W.........
E.........	E.........	E.........	E.........	E.........	E.........	E.........
S.........	S.........	S.........	S.........	S.........	S.........	S.........

22	23	24	25	26	27	28
W.........	W.........	W.........	W.........	W.........	W.........	W.........
E.........	E.........	E.........	E.........	E.........	E.........	E.........
S.........	S.........	S.........	S.........	S.........	S.........	S.........

29	30	31	Shade in each day and feel free to use more than one colour for each day!
W.........	W.........	W.........	
E.........	E.........	E.........	
S.........	S.........	S.........	

KEY
W - WEATHER
E - EXERCISE
S - SOCIAL

Sleep

Shade in the squares for each night and use the space below to record any relevant notes

HOURS →

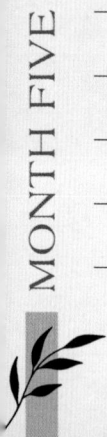

DATE ↓

	1	2	3	4	5	6	7	8	9+
1									
2									
3									
4									
5									
6									
7									
8									
9									
10									
11									
12									
13									
14									
15									
16									
17									
18									
19									
20									
21									
22									
23									
24									
25									
26									
27									
28									
29									
30									
31									

MONTH FIVE

TECH AND SLEEP

Modern technology can have a great impact on the quality of your sleep and moods. We have some tips you can try to cut down how much your devices affect your sleep

✦

BLUE LIGHT

The blue light emitted from your devices and TV has been shown to impact your body's ability to produce the hormone melatonin, which is what makes you feel relaxed and ready for sleep. If you're looking at devices too close to bedtime, you will take longer to fall asleep. You can buy blue light-blocking glasses if you do want to use devices in the evening, and many smartphones have blue light filters in their Settings menu.

✦

ONE-HOUR RULE

If possible, put devices away an hour before your bedtime. This gives you time to disengage from them and start to feel more relaxed. Ideally, these devices would be put away in another room, not your bedroom, to remove the temptation to check them.

✦

DON'T TOUCH

Once you've gone to bed and put your devices away, don't look at them until the morning. It can be tempting if you're wide awake in the middle of the night to check your messages or social media, but this will only keep you awake for longer.

✦

TECH STIMULATION

Devices stimulate your brain and make it more active, which is another reason why using devices before bed can prevent you from falling asleep easily. You should engage in tasks that are more mindful instead, as this will help relax your brain before bed.

Diet & Nutrition

Tick the squares for each day of the month. At the end of the month, look at this page alongside the 'Monthly Overview' to see if you spot any patterns

DATE ↓

Date	Breakfast	Lunch	Dinner	2x Healthy Snacks	Vegetables	Fruit	Good Fats	Protein	Wholegrains	At Least 2 Litres of Water	Unhealthy Snacks	More Than 4 Caffeinated Drinks	Alcohol	Vitamins/Supplements
1														
2														
3														
4														
5														
6														
7														
8														
9														
10														
11														
12														
13														
14														
15														
16														
17														
18														
19														
20														
21														
22														
23														
24														
25														
26														
27														
28														
29														
30														
31														

MONTH FIVE

HOW TO MANAGE CRAVINGS

What foods we crave and when we crave them can reflect our current mood. However, we often crave foods that don't support our health and can actually make our mood worse. Here are some tips to manage cravings

DRINK WATER

When you're craving a certain food, try having a big glass of cold water. Cravings are often an emotional requirement rather than due to hunger, so the drink can fill our bellies and tell our brain that we don't need food. Drink it slowly and it should help you ride out your craving until it's gone.

DISTRACT YOURSELF

When you start craving an unhealthy food, try to distract yourself with something else instead. Maybe you could go for a walk, read a book, or put on some music. If you're at work, you could try saying that you'll work on a particular task before deciding on whether to get what you're craving – hopefully by the time the task is done, the craving will have passed.

EAT REGULAR MEALS

If you're hungry, you're more likely to crave foods, and particularly foods that are high in sugar and fat to give you an instant sense of satisfaction. Try to eat balanced foods regularly throughout the day so you don't reach the point where you're so hungry you give in to temptation.

NOTICE YOUR TRIGGERS

Be aware of your cravings and think about what's triggering them. Sometimes this level of mindfulness is all you need to resist the craving. Acknowledge the craving – for example, 'I know I'm craving chocolate right now because I am feeling stressed' – and then try to think of a better solution for the cause behind the craving.

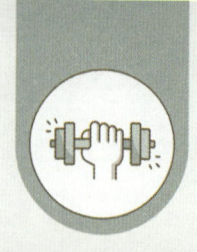

Physical Health

You can use words or emoji-style pictures to fill this bit in!

Keep track of your fitness for the month...

DATE	EXERCISE	HOW I FELT BEFORE, DURING AND AFTERWARDS	

◊ How has your general physical health been this month? Any illnesses, injuries or aches and pains worth noting?

_____
_____
_____

MONTH FIVE

PLAN YOUR EXERCISE

Planning when you are going to fit in exercise can make you more likely to stick to it. We have some top tips to help you plan, as well as space to jot down your own ideas

DIARISE YOUR EXERCISE
Write your planned exercise on your calendar or in your diary so you see it in black and white. This gives it more importance in your brain, like any other appointment, so you're more likely to stick to it. If you're new to exercise, start with planning one or two sessions a week and build up from there.

DAILY MOVEMENT
Fit your exercise in around daily tasks – little chunks throughout the day triggered by something you usually do will soon become habit and every little helps. For example, you could do some squats while brushing your teeth, or do a short stretch routine while brewing your morning coffee.

Use this space to write down some ways you can fit exercise into your current life

_____

_____

_____

_____

_____

Mental Health

◇ Write down 5 things that have made you happy this month

_____
_____
_____
_____
_____

◇ Write down 5 things that have negatively impacted your mental health this month

_____
_____
_____
_____
_____

◇ What have you done to relax this month?

_____
_____

◇ What have you done to have fun this month?

_____
_____

MONTH FIVE

COMMON MENTAL HEALTH CONDITIONS

Sometimes our low moods won't lift and this can be a sign of a mental health condition. This page gives you a short overview of some of the most common conditions

✳

DEPRESSION

It's normal to have periods of feeling down or low, but if this persists, you could be depressed. Sometimes there is an obvious trigger (like a bereavement or change in circumstances), a family history of mental unwellness, or there can be no particular cause. You should talk to a doctor if you think you're depressed; treatment ranges from lifestyle changes to talking therapies and medication. Depression is just like any other illness and nothing to be ashamed of, but it is important to get the right help.

✳

ANXIETY

Generalised anxiety disorder is when you feel anxious more than usual and it is affecting your daily life. Symptoms can include feeling restless, an ongoing sense of dread, feeling jittery or on edge, feeling irritable, mood swings and difficulty concentrating. Anxiety can also cause physical symptoms, such as dizziness, tiredness, a shortness of breath, feeling sick or headaches. Again, it's important to see a doctor to ensure you get help to cope with anxiety.

✳

STRESS

We all get stressed from time to time, but if stress builds up and continues over a long period of time, it can really affect your day-to-day life. Stress can lead to a low mood, as well as contribute to other mental health conditions. You might find it hard to concentrate or make decisions, as well as feeling overwhelmed a lot of the time. Stress can also impact on behaviour, including indulging in unhealthy practices such as smoking, drinking or eating more than usual.

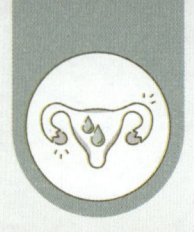

Menstrual Health

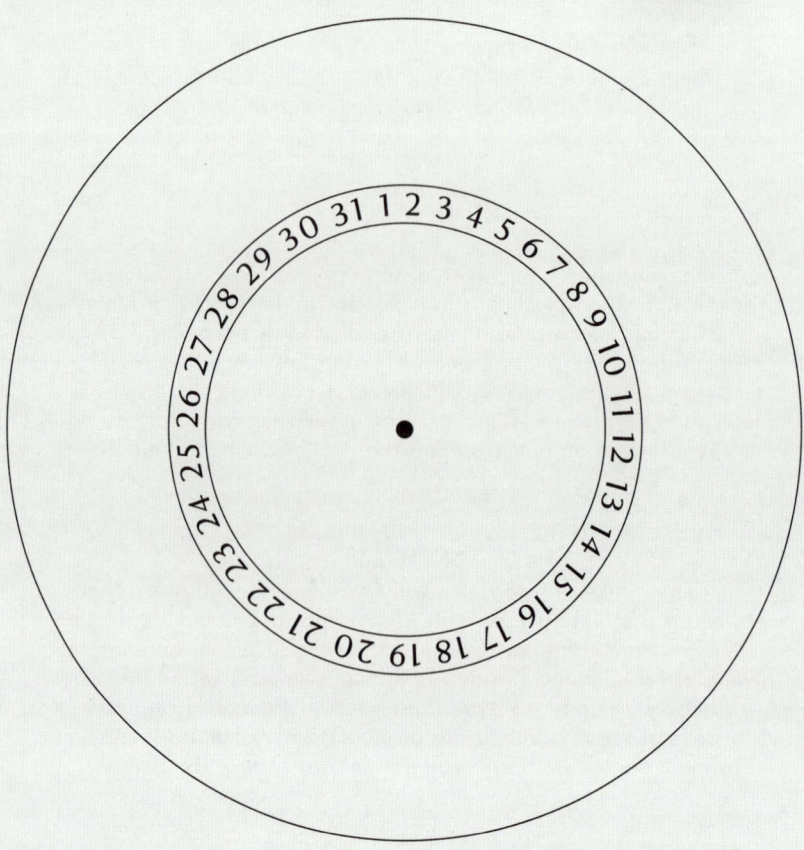

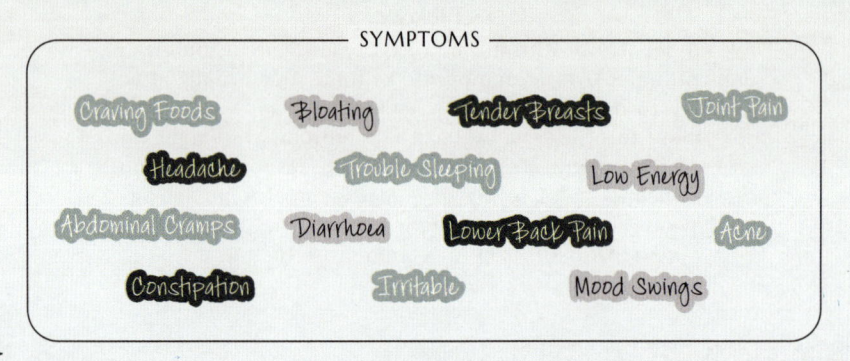

See page 7 on how to fill in the tracker

29 30 31 1 2 3 4 5 6 7 8 9 10 11 12 13 14 15 16 17 18 19 20 21 22 23 24 25 26 27 28

---- SYMPTOMS ----

Craving Foods · Bloating · Tender Breasts · Joint Pain
Headache · Trouble Sleeping · Low Energy
Abdominal Cramps · Diarrhoea · Lower Back Pain · Acne
Constipation · Irritable · Mood Swings

MONTH FIVE

ALL ABOUT PERIODS

Menstruation is the first phase of a new cycle, starting from the day you get your period and lasting for around three to seven days. Here are some tips to help you understand more about what it means for you and your moods

✷

WHAT HAPPENS
Menstruation, or your period, is the natural result of an egg being released in your body but not fertilised. It refers to the release of blood and the unfertilised egg through a woman's vagina. The blood is usually heaviest for the first two days, but everyone varies. You can expect to lose somewhere between 5 to 12 teaspoons of blood during your period, though it can be more for some women.

✷

CHEMICAL CHANGES
When you start your period, your oestrogen and progesterone levels start to drop. This change in hormone levels can have a big impact on your mood and emotions. You may experience a low mood or mood swings, particularly in the first few days of your period.

✷

MOOD CHANGES
As we mentioned in the tip above, your mood might lower due to the hormonal changes in your body, but you may find your mood is impacted by the physical impact of having your period too. If you experience pain or cramping, this can make you feel sad or low, and you might also be frustrated and irritable if you can't take part in your usual activities at this time.

✷

DON'T COMPARE
Periods vary from woman to woman, and from cycle to cycle, so it's important to not compare yourself to others. You may see some women carrying on with their usual life throughout their cycle with no impact, while you are curled up under a blanket feeling sad. Learn what's normal for you and what to expect each month.

Sociability

◇ Who have you seen this month outside of your household and workplace? Make a note of how these interactions made you feel

PERSON	WHEN/WHERE	HOW IT MADE YOU FEEL

◇ Make a note of any days you've felt lonely

_____
_____

◇ Has anyone been demanding of your time this month? Make a note of how it made you feel

_____
_____

MONTH FIVE

SOCIAL STRUGGLES

We might not all find it easy to be sociable, whether that's through worry and anxiety, a change in circumstances or feeling lonely. We have some tips to help identify your social concerns

LONELINESS

Loneliness is a feeling of sadness that comes from not having meaningful contact with friends or social groups. It's not just about being alone – many people can be alone and quite content. You can also feel lonely even if you have lots of friends and family around you. But if you're feeling sad and have a low mood because you're not getting enough social contact (whatever that means to you), then this should be addressed, and we have some activities in this journal to help.

SOCIAL ANXIETY

Social anxiety is a fear of social situations that can be overwhelming and last for a long time. Many of us are shy about social situations, and that is normal, but social anxiety is different and can have a big impact on your life. If you feel like anxiety is impacting your social health and moods, it is worth chatting to your doctor for advice.

LIFE CHANGES

Certain life changes can affect your social life, even if you once had a very healthy social life. For example, a new parent can suddenly find themselves quite lonely and unable to join friends on their usual activities. Other changes include retirement, lifestyle changes (for example, deciding to give up alcohol or drastically changing your diet) or moving to a new location. It's important to be aware of these triggers and make a new social plan to increase your contact within new social circles.

MONTHLY OVERVIEW

MONTH SIX

- Month _____   • Year _____

Notes

1	2	3	4	5	6	7
W.........	W.........	W.........	W.........	W.........	W.........	W.........
E.........	E.........	E.........	E.........	E.........	E.........	E.........
S.........	S.........	S.........	S.........	S.........	S.........	S.........

8	9	10	11	12	13	14
W.........	W.........	W.........	W.........	W.........	W.........	W.........
E.........	E.........	E.........	E.........	E.........	E.........	E.........
S.........	S.........	S.........	S.........	S.........	S.........	S.........

15	16	17	18	19	20	21
W.........	W.........	W.........	W.........	W.........	W.........	W.........
E.........	E.........	E.........	E.........	E.........	E.........	E.........
S.........	S.........	S.........	S.........	S.........	S.........	S.........

22	23	24	25	26	27	28
W.........	W.........	W.........	W.........	W.........	W.........	W.........
E.........	E.........	E.........	E.........	E.........	E.........	E.........
S.........	S.........	S.........	S.........	S.........	S.........	S.........

29	30	31
W.........	W.........	W.........
E.........	E.........	E.........
S.........	S.........	S.........

KEY
W - WEATHER
E - EXERCISE
S - SOCIAL

Shade in each day and feel free to use more than one colour for each day!

Sleep

Shade in the squares for each night and use the space below to record any relevant notes

MONTH SIX

HOURS →

DATE

WHAT'S AFFECTING YOUR SLEEP?

There are a lot of different things that can impact your sleep. On this page, you have space to think about the key factors that are affecting your sleep quality

✦

Rate each of these factors for how much you think they impact on your sleep quality. Be honest with your ratings and this will help you to identify the things that most affect you

	Doesn't impact my sleep at all		Neutral		Impacts my sleep a great deal
USE OF TECHNOLOGY	1	2	3	4	5
BEDROOM ENVIRONMENT	1	2	3	4	5
COMFORT OF BED	1	2	3	4	5
LIGHT IN BEDROOM	1	2	3	4	5
ALCOHOL BEFORE BED	1	2	3	4	5
CAFFEINE BEFORE BED	1	2	3	4	5
STRESS/WORRY	1	2	3	4	5
TEMPERATURE OF BEDROOM	1	2	3	4	5
EXERCISE BEFORE BED	1	2	3	4	5
WORKING BEFORE BED	1	2	3	4	5
OTHER _____ (WRITE IN YOUR OWN FACTOR)	1	2	3	4	5

Diet & Nutrition

Tick the squares for each day of the month. At the end of the month, look at this page alongside the 'Monthly Overview' to see if you spot any patterns

DATE →

Date	Breakfast	Lunch	Dinner	2x Healthy Snacks	Vegetables	Fruit	Good Fats	Protein	Wholegrains	At Least 2 Litres of Water	Unhealthy Snacks	More Than 4 Caffeinated Drinks	Alcohol	Vitamins/Supplements
1														
2														
3														
4														
5														
6														
7														
8														
9														
10														
11														
12														
13														
14														
15														
16														
17														
18														
19														
20														
21														
22														
23														
24														
25														
26														
27														
28														
29														
30														
31														

MONTH SIX

FOOD AND MOOD

When we feel a certain way, we might crave certain foods. It's a good idea to be able to recognise your triggers, so use this page to write down any time you're craving something and how you're feeling at the time. You might be able to identify a pattern

WHAT KIND OF FOOD AM I CRAVING?	HOW AM I FEELING RIGHT NOW?

Physical Health

You can use words or emoji-style pictures to fill this bit in!

Keep track of your fitness for the month...

DATE	EXERCISE	HOW I FELT BEFORE, DURING AND AFTERWARDS

◊ How has your general physical health been this month? Any illnesses, injuries or aches and pains worth noting?

_____
_____
_____

MONTH SIX

ENJOY YOUR ACTIVITY

Exercise and fitness should be fun! This page will help you to think about the things you enjoy doing and that will support your physical health goals

DO WHAT YOU LOVE

If you're looking to improve your physical health, find an activity that you love to do. This will make you more likely to stick at it, plus when you're enjoying it, that will lift your mood too. On the flipside, if you're not enjoying something, you don't have to keep at it – fitness should be enjoyable if you find the right activity.

OUTSIDE THE BOX

Exercise and fitness don't have to be about taking part in a traditional sport. Anything that involves moving your body can count! Even if you're dancing around your living room, doing active videogames or jumping on a trampoline, this all helps towards lifting your physical health and your mood.

Make a list of all the activities you would like to try. From paddleboarding to Pilates, running to rounders, anything goes!

_____
_____
_____
_____
_____
_____

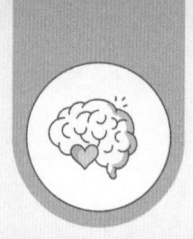

Mental Health

◇ Write down 5 things that have made you happy this month

___

◇ Write down 5 things that have negatively impacted your mental health this month

___

◇ What have you done to relax this month?

___

◇ What have you done to have fun this month?

___

MONTH SIX

COPING STRATEGIES

When we are struggling with our mental health, whether in the short term or long term, there are some techniques that can help. We explore a few of these on this page

✴

SET SOME GOALS
Working towards goals can help you to cope with mental health problems. Even if your first goal is to simply get up and get dressed, or go for a walk around the block, achieving this can give you a boost. You could try making a to-do list, but be careful not to overfill it, as this could create more worry and anxiety.

✴

EXERCISE
It's well known that exercise can affect our mental health and moods. We look at exercise in more detail in the Physical Health section of this journal. When you're feeling low, it's worth trying to do something active, even if it's just ten minutes of walking or a short yoga flow.

✴

MEDITATE
Spending some time in peace with your thoughts through a guided meditation can help to still your mind and give you a sense of calmness. This can help to pause rushing thoughts and enable you to think more rationally. We'll look at meditation and mindfulness a little further on in this journal.

✴

GET OUTSIDE
Getting outside is the simplest thing you can do to boost your mental health and mood. This could be simply sitting in your garden or a local park, or going for a walk or run. Some days you might find the thought of going out just too hard, so even if you can open the curtains and windows to get some fresh air, this is a great start.

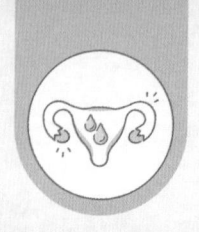

Menstrual Health

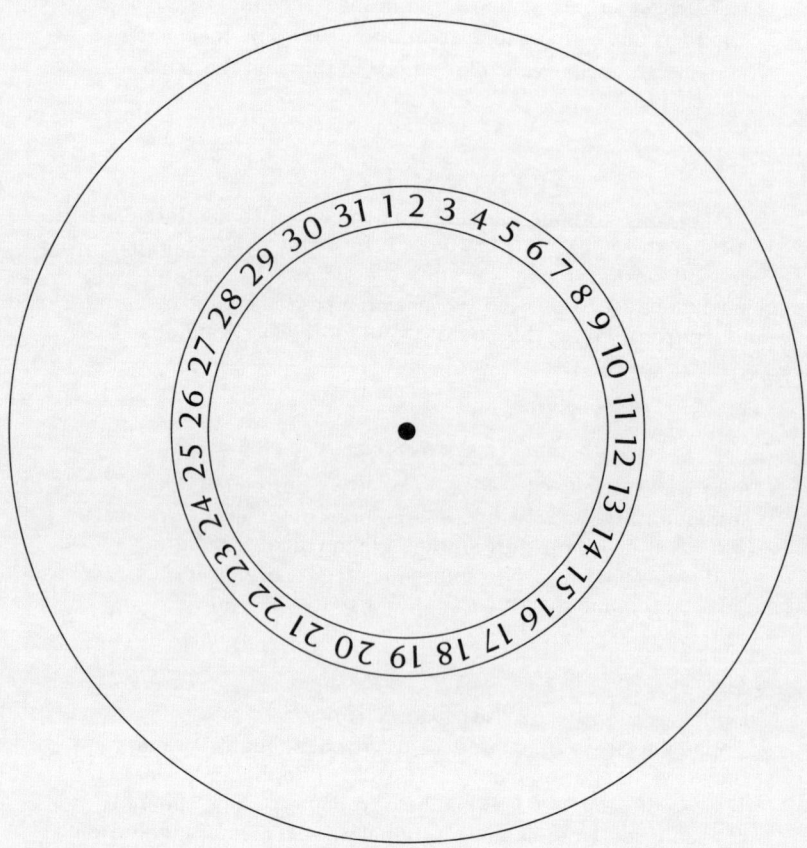

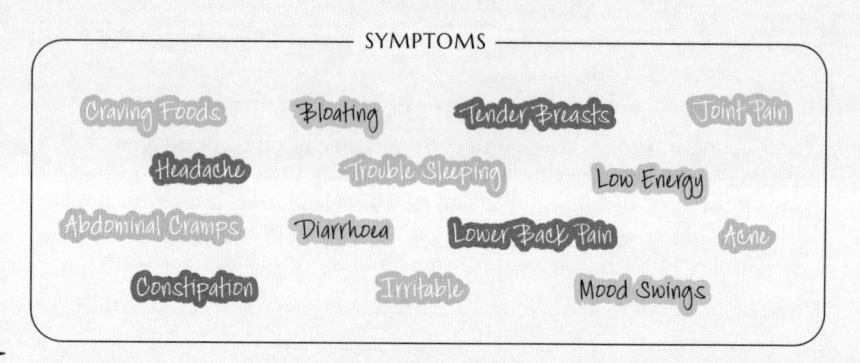

See page 7 on how to fill in the tracker

Cycle day tracker: 1–31

SYMPTOMS

- Craving Foods
- Bloating
- Tender Breasts
- Joint Pain
- Headache
- Trouble Sleeping
- Low Energy
- Abdominal Cramps
- Diarrhoea
- Lower Back Pain
- Acne
- Constipation
- Irritable
- Mood Swings

MONTH SIX

HOW YOUR PERIOD AFFECTS YOU

On this page you will be able to build up a picture of how your period affects you personally. Understanding how you feel can help you stay on top of your moods

✦

Tick the boxes for the statements that are true for you during your period

---

☐ I CAN'T EXERCISE AS MUCH AS USUAL

☐ I FEEL SAD/LOW A LOT OF THE TIME

☐ I EXPERIENCE A LOT OF PAIN

☐ I DON'T FEEL LIKE SOCIALISING WITH OTHERS

☐ I STRUGGLE WITH MY ENERGY LEVELS

☐ I FIND IT HARD TO SLEEP PROPERLY

☐ I AM FRUSTRATED BY THE THINGS I CAN'T DO

☐ I AM MORE ANXIOUS THAN USUAL

☐ HAVING MY PERIOD AFFECTS MY DAY-TO-DAY LIFESTYLE

☐ MY APPETITE CHANGES

Sociability

◊ Who have you seen this month outside of your household and workplace? Make a note of how these interactions made you feel

PERSON	WHEN/WHERE	HOW IT MADE YOU FEEL

◊ Make a note of any days you've felt lonely

_____

_____

◊ Has anyone been demanding of your time this month? Make a note of how it made you feel

_____

_____

SOCIAL PRESCRIPTION

Use this space to write yourself a prescription for what you think you need to do to improve your social health and increase your social activities

✶

This prescription will be personal to you, but you could include things like 'Arrange to meet with a friend for coffee once a fortnight' or 'Attend a group exercise class twice a week'.

Overview of social issues and problems	My prescription to improve social health

Signed: Date:

MONTHLY OVERVIEW

MONTH SEVEN

- Month _____ - Year _____

Notes

1	2	3	4	5	6	7
W.........	W.........	W.........	W.........	W.........	W.........	W.........
E.........	E.........	E.........	E.........	E.........	E.........	E.........
S.........	S.........	S.........	S.........	S.........	S.........	S.........
8	9	10	11	12	13	14
W.........	W.........	W.........	W.........	W.........	W.........	W.........
E.........	E.........	E.........	E.........	E.........	E.........	E.........
S.........	S.........	S.........	S.........	S.........	S.........	S.........
15	16	17	18	19	20	21
W.........	W.........	W.........	W.........	W.........	W.........	W.........
E.........	E.........	E.........	E.........	E.........	E.........	E.........
S.........	S.........	S.........	S.........	S.........	S.........	S.........
22	23	24	25	26	27	28
W.........	W.........	W.........	W.........	W.........	W.........	W.........
E.........	E.........	E.........	E.........	E.........	E.........	E.........
S.........	S.........	S.........	S.........	S.........	S.........	S.........
29	30	31	Shade in each day and feel free to use more than one colour for each day!			
W.........	W.........	W.........				
E.........	E.........	E.........				
S.........	S.........	S.........				

KEY

W - WEATHER
E - EXERCISE
S - SOCIAL

Sleep

Shade in the squares for each night and use the space below to record any relevant notes

HOURS →

DATE

MONTH SEVEN

DRINKS AND SLEEP

Both caffeine and alcohol can affect your quality of sleep, so it's worth trying to limit these if you want to get a restful night

CAFFEINE

The half-life of caffeine is about four to six hours. This means that any caffeine you have during the afternoon will still be present in your system in the evening when you're trying to go to sleep. Try to have no more caffeine after midday; switch to decaffeinated or herbal teas instead.

ALCOHOL

Alcohol has a sedative effect so it might help you get off to sleep. However, it can affect your usual cycles of sleep throughout the night and disrupt the balance of REM sleep, leaving you feeling more tired and in a lower mood than usual. It's best not to drink alcohol regularly before bed.

CAFFEINE TRACKER

Track your last caffeine drink and sleep quality for a week to see if a pattern emerges.

DATE	TIME OF LAST CAFFEINATED DRINK	HOW I SLEPT

Diet & Nutrition

Tick the squares for each day of the month. At the end of the month, look at this page alongside the 'Monthly Overview' to see if you spot any patterns

DATE ↓

Date	BREAKFAST	LUNCH	DINNER	2X HEALTHY SNACKS	VEGETABLES	FRUIT	GOOD FATS	PROTEIN	WHOLEGRAINS	AT LEAST 2 LITRES OF WATER	UNHEALTHY SNACKS	MORE THAN 4 CAFFEINATED DRINKS	ALCOHOL	VITAMINS/SUPPLEMENTS
1														
2														
3														
4														
5														
6														
7														
8														
9														
10														
11														
12														
13														
14														
15														
16														
17														
18														
19														
20														
21														
22														
23														
24														
25														
26														
27														
28														
29														
30														
31														

MONTH SEVEN

LOW MOOD PICK-ME-UPS

We often turn to food when we're feeling angry, sad or stressed. On this page, try to think about how you can cope with these low moods by doing things that don't involve eating or drinking

✦

Example: When I'm feeling __sad__ I usually want to eat __some chocolate__, but instead I could __read a chapter of my favourite book__.

When I'm feeling _____ I usually want to eat _____, but instead I could _____.

When I'm feeling _____ I usually want to eat _____, but instead I could _____.

When I'm feeling _____ I usually want to eat _____, but instead I could _____.

When I'm feeling _____ I usually want to eat _____, but instead I could _____.

Physical Health

You can use words or emoji-style pictures to fill this bit in!

Keep track of your fitness for the month...

DATE	EXERCISE	HOW I FELT BEFORE, DURING AND AFTERWARDS

⋄ How has your general physical health been this month? Any illnesses, injuries or aches and pains worth noting?

_____
_____
_____

MONTH SEVEN

LOOKING BACK

Throughout our lives we all go through periods where we're in good physical health and poorer physical health. Use the space on this page to think about a time in your life when you felt physically good

When in your life did you feel physically at your best?

_____

_____

What were you doing at that time that made you feel physically good?

_____

_____

Is there anything from that time of your life you could replicate in your current life?

_____

_____

Has anything specific changed in your physical health since that point?

_____

_____

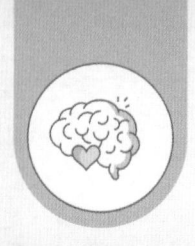

Mental Health

◇ Write down 5 things that have made you happy this month

_____

_____

_____

_____

_____

◇ Write down 5 things that have negatively impacted your mental health this month

_____

_____

_____

_____

_____

◇ What have you done to relax this month?

_____

_____

◇ What have you done to have fun this month?

_____

_____

MONTH SEVEN

MINDFULNESS

Practising mindfulness can help you with your mental health and your mood. We should all try to incorporate a small amount of mindfulness into our daily schedule

WHAT IS MINDFULNESS?

Mindfulness is about paying attention to the present moment you are in, rather than worrying about the future or dwelling on the past. It's about noticing the world around us right now and acknowledging our thoughts and feelings. In time, this awareness can help us cope better with our thoughts and improve our mood.

GETTING STARTED

There are a lot of online resources for mindfulness, with techniques you can try, as well as apps and in-person tuition. It doesn't need to be complicated, though. You can practise being mindful on your next walk – focus on what you can see around you, the colours and the textures. If you feel your mind wandering, bring it back to the present moment. With practice, it does get easier.

Use this space to write down some ways you could try to be more mindful in your daily life

_____

_____

_____

_____

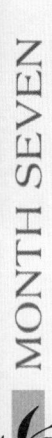

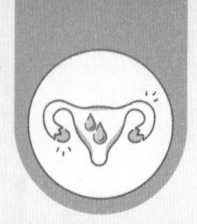

Menstrual Health

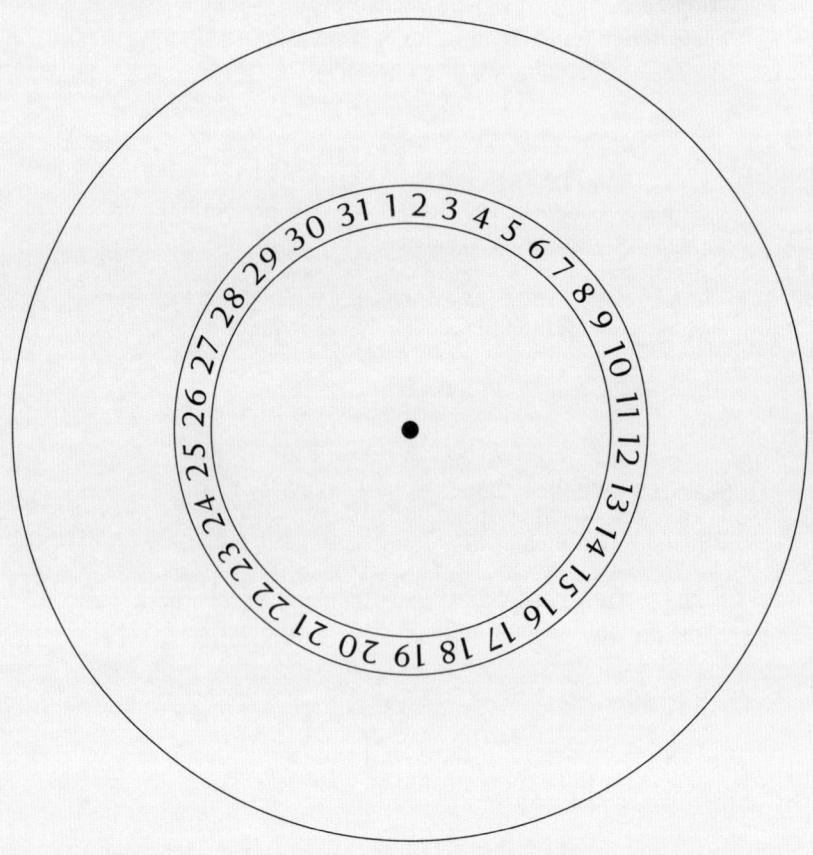

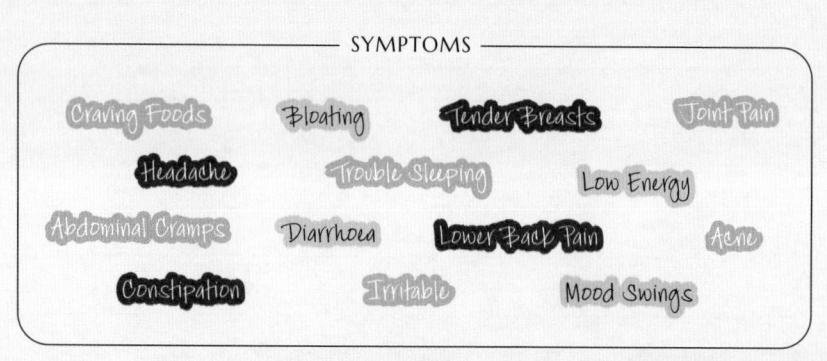

See page 7 on how to fill in the tracker

28 29 30 31 1 2 3 4 5 6 7 8 9 10 11 12 13 14 15 16 17 18 19 20 21 22 23 24 25 26 27

SYMPTOMS

Craving Foods   Bloating   Tender Breasts   Joint Pain

Headache   Trouble Sleeping   Low Energy

Abdominal Cramps   Diarrhoea   Lower Back Pain   Acne

Constipation   Irritable   Mood Swings

MONTH SEVEN

MAKING CHANGES

Use the space on this page to think about the areas that affect you most during your period and then what you could do to try to improve these in future cycles

✶

Use this space to write down what you struggle with most during your period

_____

_____

_____

_____

_____

Use this space to think of some ideas for how you could try to lessen your struggles in your next cycle

_____

_____

_____

_____

_____

_____

Sociability

◇ Who have you seen this month outside of your household and workplace? Make a note of how these interactions made you feel

PERSON	WHEN/WHERE	HOW IT MADE YOU FEEL

◇ Make a note of any days you've felt lonely

_____

_____

◇ Has anyone been demanding of your time this month? Make a note of how it made you feel

_____

_____

MONTH SEVEN

SOCIAL HURDLES

There may be obstacles standing in the way of your social health, which in turn can affect your mood. Use the space on this page to think about these hurdles in more detail

✦

What is holding you back when it comes to your social health? Write down any hurdles you face here

_____
_____
_____
_____
_____

Action points – what changes are you going to make to overcome your hurdles?

_____
_____
_____
_____
_____
_____

MONTHLY OVERVIEW

MONTH EIGHT

- Month _____   - Year _____

Notes

1	2	3	4	5	6	7
W.......	W.......	W.......	W.......	W.......	W.......	W.......
E.......	E.......	E.......	E.......	E.......	E.......	E.......
S.......	S.......	S.......	S.......	S.......	S.......	S.......

8	9	10	11	12	13	14
W.......	W.......	W.......	W.......	W.......	W.......	W.......
E.......	E.......	E.......	E.......	E.......	E.......	E.......
S.......	S.......	S.......	S.......	S.......	S.......	S.......

15	16	17	18	19	20	21
W.......	W.......	W.......	W.......	W.......	W.......	W.......
E.......	E.......	E.......	E.......	E.......	E.......	E.......
S.......	S.......	S.......	S.......	S.......	S.......	S.......

22	23	24	25	26	27	28
W.......	W.......	W.......	W.......	W.......	W.......	W.......
E.......	E.......	E.......	E.......	E.......	E.......	E.......
S.......	S.......	S.......	S.......	S.......	S.......	S.......

29	30	31				
W.......	W.......	W.......	Shade in each day and feel free to use more than one colour for each day!			
E.......	E.......	E.......				
S.......	S.......	S.......				

KEY
W - WEATHER
E - EXERCISE
S - SOCIAL

Sleep

Shade in the squares for each night and use the space below to record any relevant notes

HOURS →

DATE

MONTH EIGHT

LIFESTYLE CHANGES TO AID SLEEP

If you want to improve your sleep and your mood, then you might need to consider making some lifestyle changes

EXERCISE
Taking regular exercise has been shown to improve the quality of your sleep. However, the timing of this is important. If you do strenuous exercise too close to bedtime, you may find it hard to relax and go to sleep. Yoga and Pilates can help you to relax in the evenings and could be included in your bedtime routine.

LIMIT NAPS
When you're tired it can be tempting to have a nap, but if you nap too much, you will then find it hard to sleep at night and you could get stuck in a never-ending cycle. If you need a midday energy boost, limit a nap to no more than 20 minutes.

SLEEP FOODS
Some foods can help you get ready for sleep, particularly those with the amino acid tryptophan, which increases the production of melatonin and is an important element in balancing your mood. These foods include turkey, whole milk, oats, some nuts and bananas.

OVERCOME TIREDNESS
If you feel tired in the daytime, try to boost your energy rather than give in to a nap or rest. Going for a short walk outside can lift your energy levels, plus being outside in daylight will help your body learn when it's time to sleep. You could also try a large glass of cold water, which can also help you feel more alert.

Diet & Nutrition

Tick the squares for each day of the month. At the end of the month, look at this page alongside the 'Monthly Overview' to see if you spot any patterns

DATE ↓

DATE	BREAKFAST	LUNCH	DINNER	2X HEALTHY SNACKS	VEGETABLES	FRUIT	GOOD FATS	PROTEIN	WHOLEGRAINS	AT LEAST 2 LITRES OF WATER	MORE THAN 4 CAFFEINATED DRINKS	UNHEALTHY SNACKS	ALCOHOL	VITAMINS/SUPPLEMENTS
1														
2														
3														
4														
5														
6														
7														
8														
9														
10														
11														
12														
13														
14														
15														
16														
17														
18														
19														
20														
21														
22														
23														
24														
25														
26														
27														
28														
29														
30														
31														

MONTH EIGHT

LIFT-ME-UP LUNCHES

Use this page to think about what you'd like to achieve in your diet to help boost your moods. Setting clear goals can help you stay focused. Lunchtime is a great opportunity to get some more mood-boosting foods into your diet, but many of us skip lunch or rush it. Here are some tips to maximise your midday meal motivation when making lifestyle changes

LOVELY LEFTOVERS

A simple way to improve your lunch is to overcook at dinnertime, leaving you some nutritious leftovers for the next day's lunch. There is no thinking needed – simply pop your leftovers in a tub and warm them up (if needed) the next day for a filling and satisfying meal.

PACK YOUR LUNCH

Prepare your lunch in advance to avoid the temptations in the local shop or café! Taking a packed lunch means you know you have a balanced meal ready to eat. Even if you work from home, it can be worth making a packed lunch so you don't have to make something in a hurry.

Packed lunch inspiration! Use this space to list five packed lunches that you could prepare in advance to make your days easier

1 _____
2 _____
3 _____
4 _____
5 _____

Physical Health

You can use words or emoji-style pictures to fill this bit in!

Keep track of your fitness for the month...

DATE	EXERCISE	HOW I FELT BEFORE, DURING AND AFTERWARDS

◇ How has your general physical health been this month? Any illnesses, injuries or aches and pains worth noting?

_____

_____

_____

MONTH EIGHT

DO YOUR RESEARCH

Now you've had a chance to think about what activities you might like to try to improve your physical health, do some research about what's available to you, whether that's classes in your local area, clubs you can join or online videos to try

Something I would like to try: _____
What is available for me to support this goal?

_____

_____

Something I would like to try: _____
What is available for me to support this goal?

_____

_____

Something I would like to try: _____
What is available for me to support this goal?

_____

_____

Something I would like to try: _____
What is available for me to support this goal?

_____

_____

Mental Health

◇ Write down 5 things that have made you happy this month

_____
_____
_____
_____
_____

◇ Write down 5 things that have negatively impacted your mental health this month

_____
_____
_____
_____
_____

◇ What have you done to relax this month?

_____
_____

◇ What have you done to have fun this month?

_____
_____

MONTH EIGHT

PRACTISE MEDITATION

If you're new to meditation, try this short exercise and write down your thoughts and feelings about it at the end. Make sure you're in a quiet place where you can't be disturbed, sit comfortably and follow this guide

AN OBSERVATION MEDITATION
(FIVE TO TEN MINUTES)

- Make sure you are sitting comfortably and that there are no distractions.
- Now close your eyes and begin to take notice of your breathing.
- Breathe in deeply for a count of five, hold for a count of two, then breathe out slowly for a count of five.
- Repeat this a few times. If your mind wanders, bring it back to your counting.
- Next, focus your attention on your body. What can you feel? Are there any aches and pains? Any tension?
- Scan through your body slowly from top to bottom, asking the same questions.
- Next, observe your thoughts. Do you have any specific worries? Are you feeling happy or sad?
- Finally, return to your breathing and repeat the third step before bringing yourself back to the present and opening your eyes.

Now you have finished your short meditation, use this space to write down any notes. Was it easy or hard to stay present and focused? How did you feel after the exercise? Has your mood improved at all?

_____

_____

_____

_____

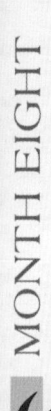

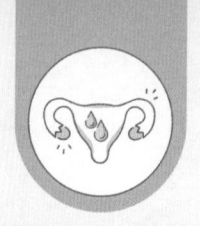

Menstrual Health

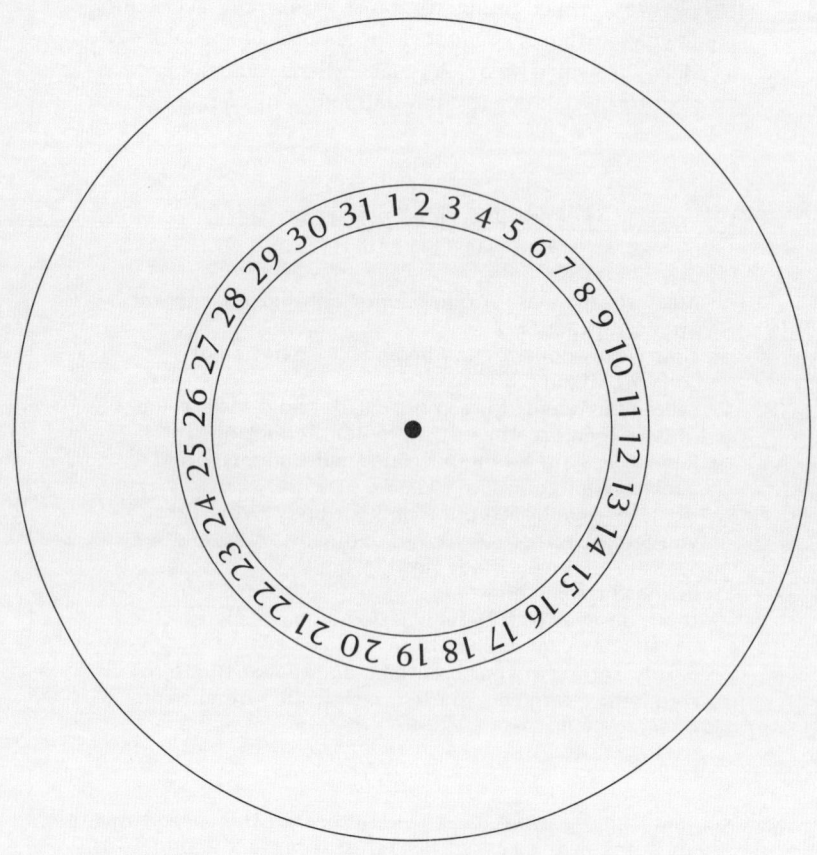

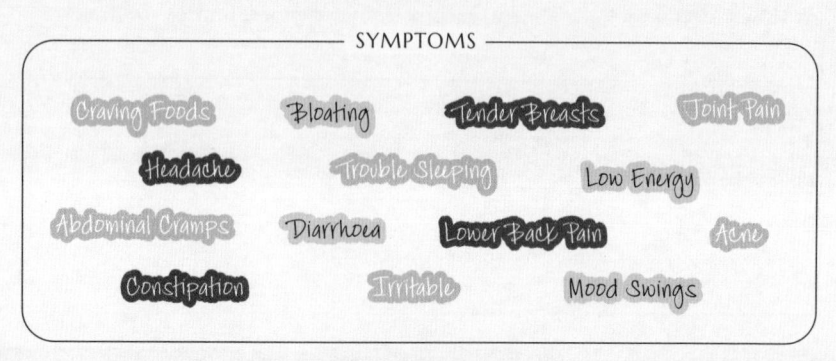

See page 7 on how to fill in the tracker

Calendar wheel: 1 2 3 4 5 6 7 8 9 10 11 12 13 14 15 16 17 18 19 20 21 22 23 24 25 26 27 28 29 30 31

SYMPTOMS

- Craving Foods
- Bloating
- Tender Breasts
- Joint Pain
- Headache
- Trouble Sleeping
- Low Energy
- Abdominal Cramps
- Diarrhoea
- Lower Back Pain
- Acne
- Constipation
- Irritable
- Mood Swings

MONTH EIGHT

OPTIMISE YOUR EXERCISE

During your period, you might not feel like exercising too much, but being active can relieve the symptoms while also giving you a much-needed mood boost

✦

GO GENTLE

You might not feel too much like doing a strenuous activity, but even something gentle can improve your mood and period symptoms. A long walk outside can be kind on your joints and make you feel better. Swimming is great for managing any pain or cramping. Yoga stretches can also relieve aches and pains, plus it's good for your mental health.

✦

BYE BYE BLOAT

Many of us experience bloating during our periods, which is not surprising as you can take on anything up to ten pounds of extra water! Exercising can help, as working up a sweat can help to get rid of some of this excess water and make you feel more comfortable around your stomach.

✦

EXERCISE AND PERIOD TRACKER

Write down any exercise you do during your period and think about how you felt afterwards. For example, you might have gone swimming and noticed a decrease in pain levels and an uplift in your mood.

DATE	EXERCISE	HOW I FELT AFTERWARDS

Sociability

◇ Who have you seen this month outside of your household and workplace? Make a note of how these interactions made you feel

PERSON	WHEN/WHERE	HOW IT MADE YOU FEEL

◇ Make a note of any days you've felt lonely

_____

_____

◇ Has anyone been demanding of your time this month? Make a note of how it made you feel

_____

_____

MONTH EIGHT

NEW SOCIAL ACTIVITIES

It can be scary to try something new with people you've never met before, but the long-term impact on your mood can make the initial jump worth it

FIND SOCIAL GROUPS

The internet is a wonderful thing when it comes to finding ways to interact with like-minded people. With a little time spent on Google or Facebook, you should be able to track down some local groups based around the hobbies and activities you enjoy or would like to try. Make a commitment to yourself to try one new group to see if you like it.

FACE YOUR FEARS

If you are afraid of a new social situation, it can be tempting to avoid them altogether. But if you want to increase your social activities, at some point you will need to try to overcome the fear. You could ask a friend to go with you to a new class for the first time, or you could start small and commit to a trial session of a new group to see if you like it.

What I would like to try: _____

What do I fear about trying it? _____

What can I do to overcome this fear? _____

What I would like to try: _____

What do I fear about trying it? _____

What can I do to overcome this fear? _____

MONTHLY OVERVIEW

MONTH NINE

◆ Month _____   ◆ Year _____

Notes

1	2	3	4	5	6	7
W........	W........	W........	W........	W........	W........	W........
E.........	E.........	E.........	E.........	E.........	E.........	E.........
S.........	S.........	S.........	S.........	S.........	S.........	S.........

8	9	10	11	12	13	14
W........	W........	W........	W........	W........	W........	W........
E.........	E.........	E.........	E.........	E.........	E.........	E.........
S.........	S.........	S.........	S.........	S.........	S.........	S.........

15	16	17	18	19	20	21
W........	W........	W........	W........	W........	W........	W........
E.........	E.........	E.........	E.........	E.........	E.........	E.........
S.........	S.........	S.........	S.........	S.........	S.........	S.........

22	23	24	25	26	27	28
W........	W........	W........	W........	W........	W........	W........
E.........	E.........	E.........	E.........	E.........	E.........	E.........
S.........	S.........	S.........	S.........	S.........	S.........	S.........

29	30	31				
W........	W........	W........	Shade in each day and feel free to use more than one colour for each day!			
E.........	E.........	E.........				
S.........	S.........	S.........				

KEY
W - WEATHER
E - EXERCISE
S - SOCIAL

Sleep

Shade in the squares for each night and use the space below to record any relevant notes

MONTH NINE

HOURS →

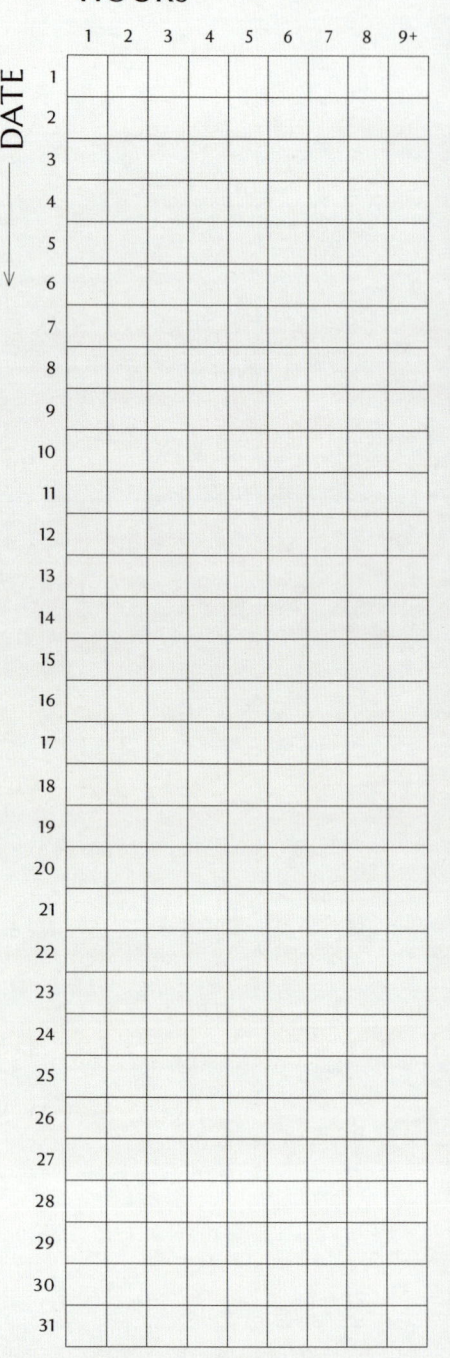

DATE ↓

Date	1	2	3	4	5	6	7	8	9+
1									
2									
3									
4									
5									
6									
7									
8									
9									
10									
11									
12									
13									
14									
15									
16									
17									
18									
19									
20									
21									
22									
23									
24									
25									
26									
27									
28									
29									
30									
31									

SETTING A ROUTINE

A bedtime routine can help you get ready for sleep and it can also help you feel calm and relaxed, lifting your mood

TAKE A BATH
When you go to sleep, your body's core temperature drops. If you include a warm bath as part of your routine, you heat your body's core temperature, then it cools again afterwards, which the brain can take as a sign that it's time to go to sleep. It's also a nice, relaxing self-care activity.

READ A BOOK
Rather than looking at electronic devices, try reading before bedtime, or any other calming hobby you enjoy, such as drawing, colouring, knitting or doing a jigsaw puzzle. This can help you to feel more mindful and focused, while also relaxing from the stresses of the day.

MEDITATE
Even if you've never tried it before, meditation can be a great part of your bedtime routine. It can help prepare your mind for sleep, as well as give you the chance to unwind before going to bed. There are meditation apps that can talk you through a pre-sleep session.

HAVE A WARM DRINK
A warm drink can help you to relax before bedtime in a similar way to a bath, by raising your body's temperature and then cooling it down. A bedtime drink that includes chamomile can help you feel more relaxed, or opt for warm milk to promote feelings of sleepiness.

Diet & Nutrition

Tick the squares for each day of the month. At the end of the month, look at this page alongside the 'Monthly Overview' to see if you spot any patterns

DATE →

	BREAKFAST	LUNCH	DINNER	2X HEALTHY SNACKS	VEGETABLES	FRUIT	GOOD FATS	PROTEIN	WHOLEGRAINS	AT LEAST 2 LITRES OF WATER	UNHEALTHY SNACKS	MORE THAN 4 CAFFEINATED DRINKS	ALCOHOL	VITAMINS/SUPPLEMENTS
1														
2														
3														
4														
5														
6														
7														
8														
9														
10														
11														
12														
13														
14														
15														
16														
17														
18														
19														
20														
21														
22														
23														
24														
25														
26														
27														
28														
29														
30														
31														

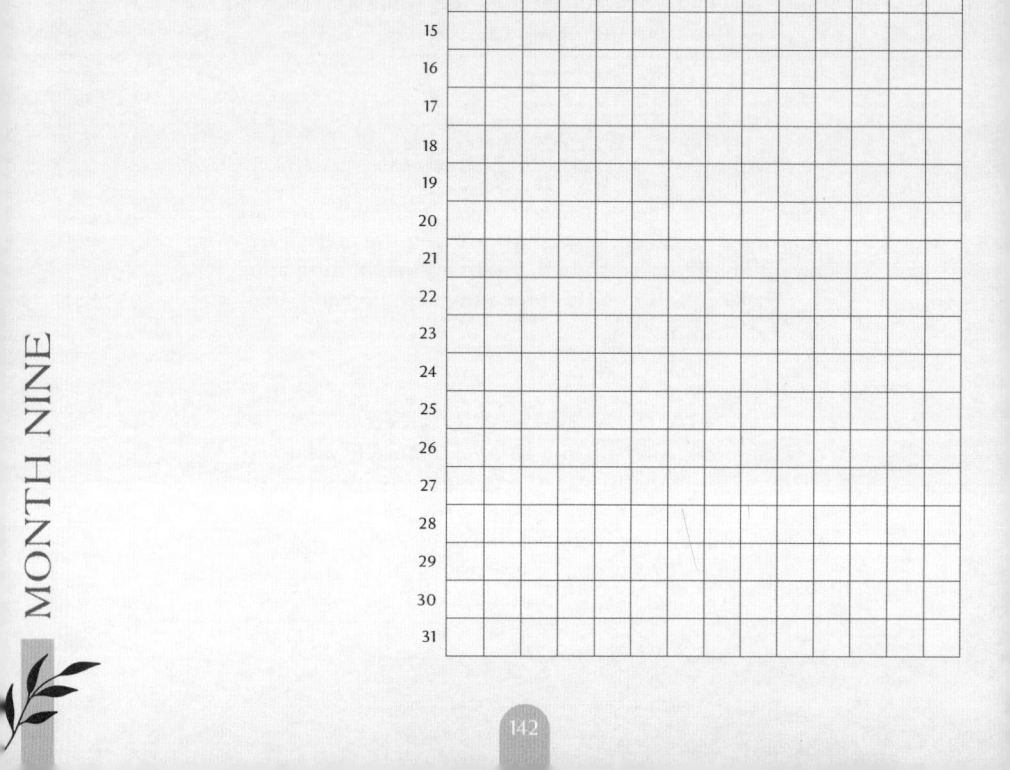

MONTH NINE

SUPER SNACKS

Snacks throughout the day are a great way to add in more amazing mood foods. Here we have some ideas to help you snack smart

NIBBLE ON NUTS

Nuts are a great mood-busting snack, as long as you go for raw ones that haven't been roasted or salted. Some nuts, like cashews and almonds, boost your serotonin levels and therefore your mood. Nuts are also a good source of healthy fats. You could also try a nut butter spread on apple slices or a crispbread as another snack option.

CHOOSE CHICKPEAS

You probably haven't thought much about snacking on chickpeas, but they are a good source of mood-friendly vitamins and minerals like B6 and magnesium. They are also high in protein, and help to elevate your serotonin and dopamine levels. Try them roasted as a snack, or use to make your own hummus.

BEAUTIFUL BERRIES

If you fancy a fruit-based snack, go for a bowl of mixed berries. They are packed with antioxidants to help your brain health and they're a good source of fibre for gut health – both things that will help you feel balanced and happy. You could even throw them in a smoothie for another snack choice.

PACK YOUR SNACKS

Prepare your snacks in advance so you always have something to hand if you feel hungry. Having an abundance of colourful, healthy snacks right in front of you will help stop you reaching for the biscuit tin.

Physical Health

You can use words or emoji-style pictures to fill this bit in!

Keep track of your fitness for the month...

DATE	EXERCISE	HOW I FELT BEFORE, DURING AND AFTERWARDS

⋄ How has your general physical health been this month? Any illnesses, injuries or aches and pains worth noting?

_____
_____
_____

MONTH NINE

LIMITATIONS TO PHYSICAL HEALTH

If you have long-term conditions that impact your physical health or limit the activity you can manage, you may need to think about how you could adapt an activity or explore new options

BE KIND

Don't be hard on yourself if there are things you feel you can't do for any reason. It's important to work within your limits so as not to overexert yourself or do yourself any physical harm. Be kind to yourself and try to focus on what you can do, rather than what you can't. If you focus on the negatives, this will impact on your mood too.

FIND A PRO

If you have a specific condition or limitation, it can be worth getting some professional help to improve your physical health. There are wellness programmes at some gyms (you may need to be referred by your doctor or hospital) that adapt to your needs, or you can find a personal trainer with specific experience to help you.

Use this activity to think about something you wish you could do but feel you are unable to, and then consider what you could do instead

Something I feel I can't do: _____

Something I could do instead: _____

Something I feel I can't do: _____

Something I could do instead: _____

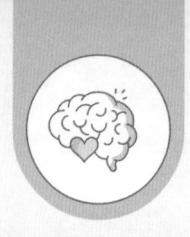

Mental Health

◇ Write down 5 things that have made you happy this month

_____

_____

_____

_____

_____

◇ Write down 5 things that have negatively impacted your mental health this month

_____

_____

_____

_____

_____

◇ What have you done to relax this month?

_____

_____

◇ What have you done to have fun this month?

_____

_____

MONTH NINE

UNDERSTAND YOUR FEELINGS

Acknowledging and noticing your feelings can make you feel more in control of them, which can help you to balance your moods

---

WRITE IT DOWN

This journal gives you space to write down your feelings and this is an important step towards good mental health. No matter what your thoughts are, try to make note of them. You may see patterns over the course of a month or spot triggers for low moods. Try to be consistent with your journalling.

TALK TO OTHERS

We don't often take time to talk about our feelings when we're with other people, but it's a really good practice. Explaining how we feel can make more sense of these emotions. Plus, sharing a worry can help it lift a little, improving our mood and mental health – as the saying goes, a problem shared is a problem halved.

ASK FOR HELP

Many of us are really bad at asking for help. This doesn't just mean medical help for a mental health condition. Sometimes you might need help with a practical concern that's worrying you, or you might have taken on too much work and need some support. Getting the right help when you need it can prevent stress and anxiety.

ACKNOWLEDGE

Be aware that you can't expect to feel happy all the time. However, you can acknowledge when you feel your mood dipping and use this as a trigger to audit your current life and see if there is anything that you could try to improve. Our moods can often reflect our lifestyle and are a good sign that something might need changing.

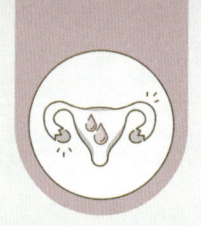

Menstrual Health

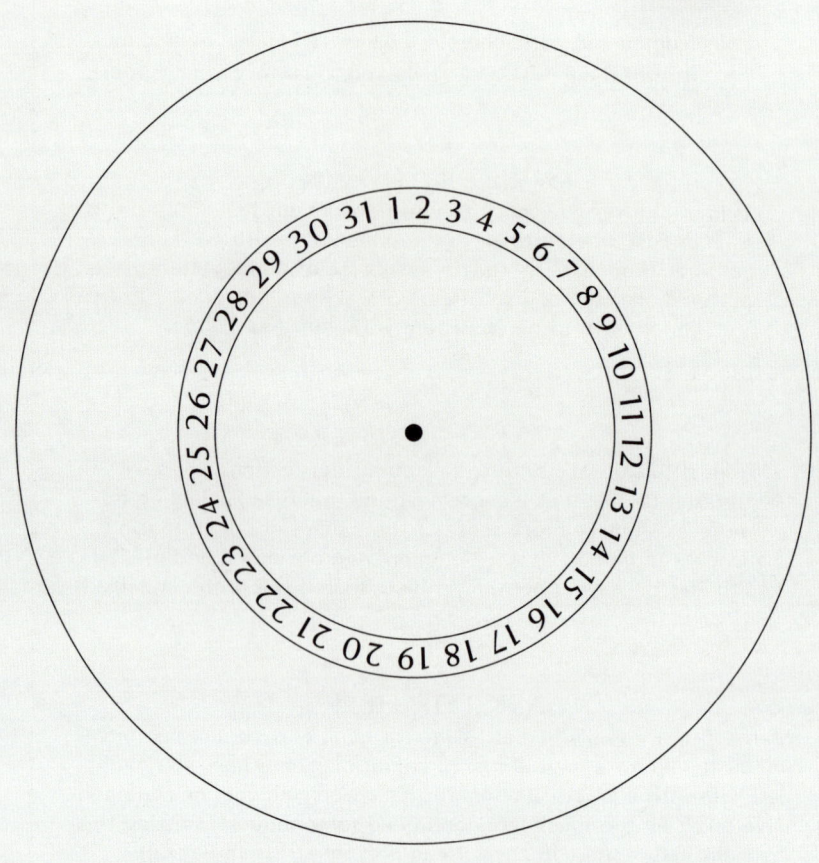

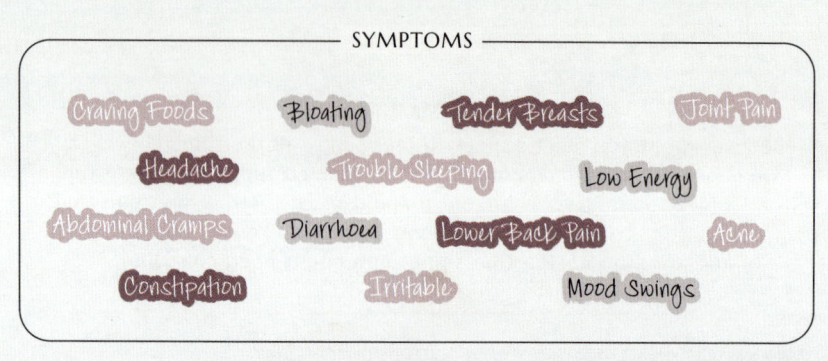

See page 7 on how to fill in the tracker

(Circular tracker with days 1–31)

— SYMPTOMS —

- Craving Foods
- Bloating
- Tender Breasts
- Joint Pain
- Headache
- Trouble Sleeping
- Low Energy
- Abdominal Cramps
- Diarrhoea
- Lower Back Pain
- Acne
- Constipation
- Irritable
- Mood Swings

MONTH NINE

EXERCISE THROUGHOUT YOUR CYCLE

You may need to adapt your fitness routine during your cycle. We have some top tips to help you understand how your cycle affects your physical performance

LOW ENERGY

During your period, your hormone levels drop and you might also be low in iron due to the blood loss. During this time, strenuous activity might be counterproductive, so consider things like yoga, which can help you to feel calmer, manage pain, be more energetic and feel uplifted.

FOLLICULAR FITNESS

The follicular phase starts from day one of your period, crossing over with the menstruation phase, but carries on for a couple of weeks. During this time, you will get a surge of oestrogen and, once you've got over the worst of your period, you should feel your energy rising. Now is a good time to increase your exercise intensity.

OVULATION EXERCISE

When you are ovulating, you might find your energy levels are at their highest so this is a great time for intense, regular exercise to make the most of those feel-good hormones. You will probably find that your performance peaks at this stage of your cycle.

EXERCISE TRACKING

The only way to know how your cycle impacts on your fitness and exercise is to write it down. If you routinely track your exercise, get in the habit of making a note of where you are in your cycle. This means that you can start to see any patterns between your cycle and your performance/energy levels.

Sociability

◇ Who have you seen this month outside of your household and workplace? Make a note of how these interactions made you feel

PERSON	WHEN/WHERE	HOW IT MADE YOU FEEL

◇ Make a note of any days you've felt lonely

_____

_____

◇ Has anyone been demanding of your time this month? Make a note of how it made you feel

_____

_____

MONTH NINE

SOCIAL BURNOUT

It is possible to over-socialise, leaving you feeling rundown and burned out. Here we have some tips if you need a break from your social life

SOCIAL EXHAUSTION

It's important to recognise the signs of social burnout so you can act quickly before it impacts too much on your mental health and mood. Symptoms include: a feeling of detachment from others; trouble sleeping; feeling low, depressed or anxious; low energy levels; headaches; mood swings and an inability to focus.

FOMO

The Fear Of Missing Out can make us attend functions that we don't want to really go to, thinking that something might happen that we won't be a part of. However, it's important to put this into perspective. Explore your feelings around an event. Do you really want to go? Or are you just afraid of missing out? What would actually happen if you missed something? Listen to your body; sometimes choosing not to go is better for our mood in the long term.

IDENTIFY TRIGGERS

Some events might cause social exhaustion more than others. Try to think about which types of events are triggers for you, and which ones enhance your social life. This will help you to prioritise those events that will support your social health, and let go of those that contribute to burnout.

SCHEDULE ALONE TIME

If you're heading into a period of busyness with lots of social functions, make sure you schedule in some alone time to balance things out. This can help you avoid the social exhaustion that can come in a busy time of life. Adequate rest is key to managing your moods when you are always on the go.

MONTHLY OVERVIEW

MONTH TEN

Month _____   Year _____

Notes
_____
_____
_____
_____
_____
_____
_____
_____
_____
_____
_____
_____
_____

1	2	3	4	5	6	7
W..... E..... S.....	W..... E..... S.....	W..... E..... S.....	W..... E..... S.....	W..... E..... S.....	W..... E..... S.....	W..... E..... S.....
8	9	10	11	12	13	14
W..... E..... S.....	W..... E..... S.....	W..... E..... S.....	W..... E..... S.....	W..... E..... S.....	W..... E..... S.....	W..... E..... S.....
15	16	17	18	19	20	21
W..... E..... S.....	W..... E..... S.....	W..... E..... S.....	W..... E..... S.....	W..... E..... S.....	W..... E..... S.....	W..... E..... S.....
22	23	24	25	26	27	28
W..... E..... S.....	W..... E..... S.....	W..... E..... S.....	W..... E..... S.....	W..... E..... S.....	W..... E..... S.....	W..... E..... S.....
29	30	31	Shade in each day and feel free to use more than one colour for each day!			
W..... E..... S.....	W..... E..... S.....	W..... E..... S.....				

KEY

W - WEATHER

E - EXERCISE

S - SOCIAL

Sleep

Shade in the squares for each night and use the space below to record any relevant notes

MONTH TEN

HOURS →

DATE ↓

Date	1	2	3	4	5	6	7	8	9+
1									
2									
3									
4									
5									
6									
7									
8									
9									
10									
11									
12									
13									
14									
15									
16									
17									
18									
19									
20									
21									
22									
23									
24									
25									
26									
27									
28									
29									
30									
31									

YOUR BEDTIME ROUTINE

Use the space on this page to plan out your new bedtime routine, thinking about all the things you want to incorporate during your evening wind-down

✴

Two hours before bedtime I will...

_____

_____

One hour before bedtime I will...

_____

_____

Thirty minutes before bedtime I will...

_____

_____

Ten minutes before bedtime I will...

_____

_____

As I go to bed I will...

_____

_____

Diet & Nutrition

Tick the squares for each day of the month. At the end of the month, look at this page alongside the 'Monthly Overview' to see if you spot any patterns

DATE

	BREAKFAST	LUNCH	DINNER	2X HEALTHY SNACKS	VEGETABLES	FRUIT	GOOD FATS	PROTEIN	WHOLEGRAINS	AT LEAST 2 LITRES OF WATER	UNHEALTHY SNACKS	MORE THAN 4 CAFFEINATED DRINKS	ALCOHOL	VITAMINS/SUPPLEMENTS
1														
2														
3														
4														
5														
6														
7														
8														
9														
10														
11														
12														
13														
14														
15														
16														
17														
18														
19														
20														
21														
22														
23														
24														
25														
26														
27														
28														
29														
30														
31														

MONTH TEN

INCREASE YOUR MOOD FOODS

Try to incorporate more mood-boosting foods into your diet. See if you can complete our bingo card – cross them off as you go!

BANANA	KALE	APPLE	ONION	GRAPES
KEFIR	BEETROOT	SWEET POTATO	WALNUTS	CHIA SEEDS
PUMPKIN SEEDS	MUSHROOMS	DARK CHOCOLATE	CHICKPEAS	EDAMAME
OATS	GREEN TEA	ORANGE	MIXED BERRIES	AVOCADO
SPINACH	TURMERIC	BRAZIL NUTS	COCONUT	ASPARAGUS

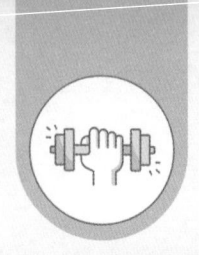

Physical Health

You can use words or emoji-style pictures to fill this bit in!

Keep track of your fitness for the month...

DATE	EXERCISE	HOW I FELT BEFORE, DURING AND AFTERWARDS

◊ How has your general physical health been this month? Any illnesses, injuries or aches and pains worth noting?

_____

_____

_____

MONTH TEN

KEEPING THE MOMENTUM

Once you start on the path towards improved physical health, it's important to keep going. We have some tips to keep you motivated

✦

ENTER AN EVENT
If you enjoy being competitive, you may like to find an event you can train for. There are all kinds of events for activities such as walking, running, hiking, cycling, swimming, dancing etc. This can give you an end goal to focus on, which can be great motivation.

✦

PROGRESSIVE PLANS
If you feel like you have hit a plateau with your physical health, you might like to find a programme to help you progress further. For example, if you like running and you have recently completed a 5K run, you could look for a plan to take you from 5K to 10K for example, or to run your 5K faster. This idea can be applied to any form of exercise.

✦

MIX IT UP
Rather than focusing on just one kind of fitness activity, try to combine a few. This will stop you from getting bored as well as improving your physical health in lots of different ways. Try to include some high-intensity activity, some gentler cardio, some strength work and some stretching/yoga/Pilates.

✦

JOIN A CLUB
Doing an activity with other people can be a great way to ensure you keep at it. This could be signing up to a gym or attending classes regularly, becoming a member of a sport-specific club, or joining a team. Not only will your mood benefit from the physical activity itself, but you'll also feel uplifted by the community aspect.

Mental Health

◇ Write down 5 things that have made you happy this month

_____
_____
_____
_____
_____

◇ Write down 5 things that have negatively impacted your mental health this month

_____
_____
_____
_____
_____

◇ What have you done to relax this month?

_____
_____

◇ What have you done to have fun this month?

_____
_____

MONTH TEN

VISUALISATION

Pictures and photos can be a powerful prompt for our mental health. That's why mood boards can be a great tool to help visualise a lifestyle change or solve a problem. This page gives you space for your own visual aid

What makes you happy? Is it a place or a person or a colour? Use this area to draw something that makes you happy. If you're not feeling creative, you could stick a photo or magazine clipping here instead

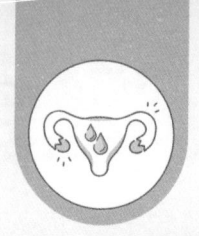

Menstrual Health

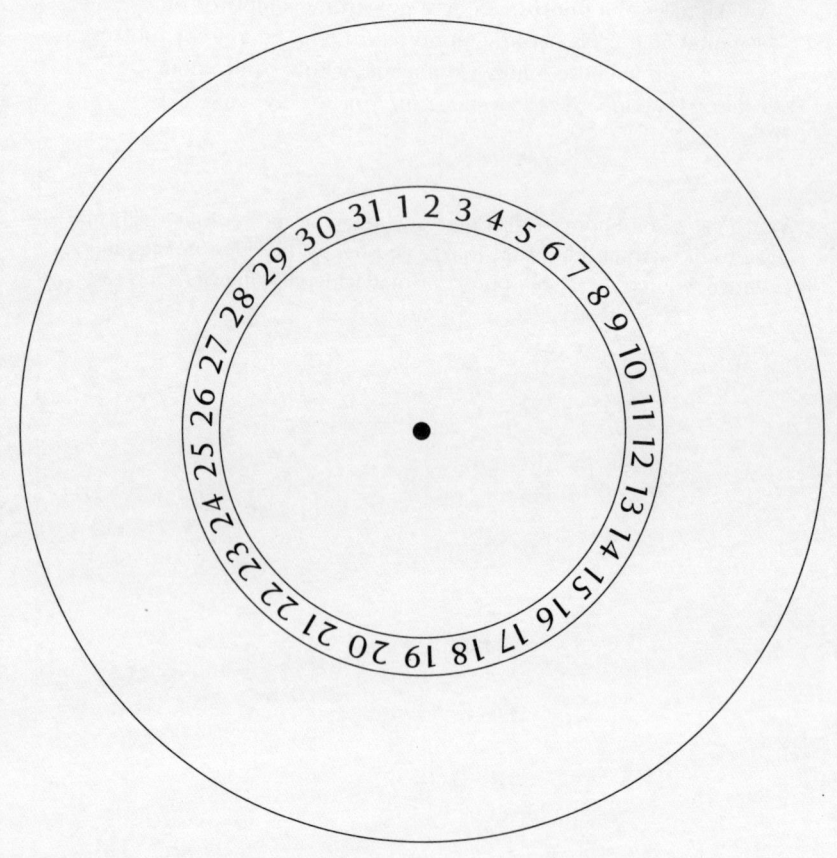

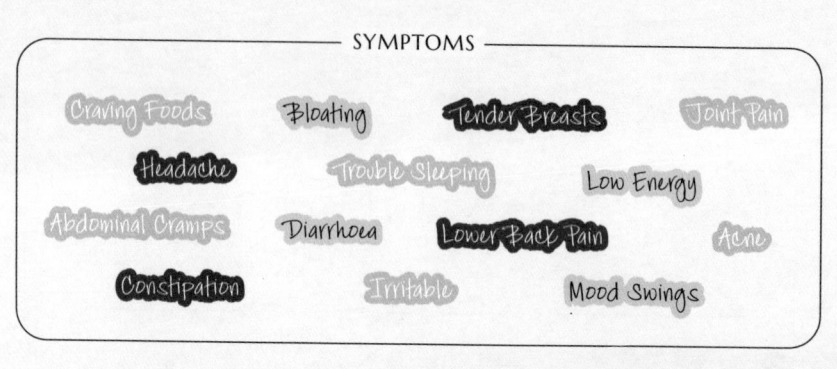

See page 7 on how to fill in the tracker

31 1 2 3 4 5 6 7 8 9 10 11 12 13 14 15 16 17 18 19 20 21 22 23 24 25 26 27 28 29 30

SYMPTOMS

- Craving Foods
- Bloating
- Tender Breasts
- Joint Pain
- Headache
- Trouble Sleeping
- Low Energy
- Abdominal Cramps
- Diarrhoea
- Lower Back Pain
- Acne
- Constipation
- Irritable
- Mood Swings

MONTH TEN

CONSIDER THE MENOPAUSE

No matter how old you are now, menopause is something that is on the horizon and is a natural part of life for a woman. On this page, we explain the different stages of menopause

✦

PREMENOPAUSE
Premenopause comes before perimenopause and menopause, and is the period of time before a woman starts to experience menopausal symptoms. From around your mid-20s, your fertility will peak and then start to slowly decline. During premenopause you shouldn't experience any symptoms, but inside your body your hormone levels are slowly starting to shift.

✦

PERIMENOPAUSE
This next stage normally begins in your 40s, although some women will find symptoms starting earlier than that. This is a transitionary phase towards menopause, and there are a lot of common signs and symptoms (see our next activity, later in the journal). Perimenopause is caused by a drop in oestrogen levels, and symptoms tend to worsen as hormones decline. This stage can last eight to ten years.

✦

MENOPAUSE
The usual age for menopause is 45-55, but it can occur sooner or later than this. The average age of reaching menopause is around 51. You are considered to be in menopause after 12 consecutive months without a period. At this point, you should reach 'ovarian follicular depletion', resulting in low oestrogen levels, which may result in low moods or mood swings.

✦

EARLY MENOPAUSE
It is possible to experience menopause earlier than expected. This could be due to lifestyle factors (smoking, for example), genetics (if you have a family history of early menopause), certain autoimmune disorders, medical menopause (such as certain hormone-blocking medications or via a hysterectomy) or as a side effect of some treatments (such as chemotherapy). Your doctor can advise you in these circumstances.

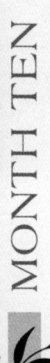

Sociability

◇ Who have you seen this month outside of your household and workplace? Make a note of how these interactions made you feel

PERSON	WHEN/WHERE	HOW IT MADE YOU FEEL

◇ Make a note of any days you've felt lonely

_____

_____

◇ Has anyone been demanding of your time this month? Make a note of how it made you feel

_____

_____

YOUR SOCIAL LIMITS

This page gives you a chance to think about what types of social events leave you feeling tired and low, and which ones make you feel energised and happy

Rate each of these factors for how much you think they impact on your social health. Be honest with your ratings and this will help you to identify the things that most affect you

	Leaves me feeling tired/ exhausted		Neutral		Makes me feel energised and happy
LARGE PARTIES	1	2	3	4	5
WORK/NETWORKING EVENTS	1	2	3	4	5
GROUP EXERCISE CLASSES	1	2	3	4	5
ATTENDING CONCERTS/SHOWS	1	2	3	4	5
MEAL OUT WITH FRIENDS	1	2	3	4	5
NIGHT IN WITH FRIENDS	1	2	3	4	5
GOING TO PUBS/CLUBS	1	2	3	4	5
WALKING/RUNNING WITH A FRIEND	1	2	3	4	5
ALL-DAY EVENTS/FESTIVALS	1	2	3	4	5
MINI-BREAKS/DAY TRIPS WITH OTHERS	1	2	3	4	5
OTHER _____ (WRITE IN YOUR OWN FACTOR)	1	2	3	4	5

MONTHLY OVERVIEW

MONTH ELEVEN

- Month _____ • Year _____

Notes

1	2	3	4	5	6	7
W......	W......	W......	W......	W......	W......	W......
E......	E......	E......	E......	E......	E......	E......
S......	S......	S......	S......	S......	S......	S......

8	9	10	11	12	13	14
W......	W......	W......	W......	W......	W......	W......
E......	E......	E......	E......	E......	E......	E......
S......	S......	S......	S......	S......	S......	S......

15	16	17	18	19	20	21
W......	W......	W......	W......	W......	W......	W......
E......	E......	E......	E......	E......	E......	E......
S......	S......	S......	S......	S......	S......	S......

22	23	24	25	26	27	28
W......	W......	W......	W......	W......	W......	W......
E......	E......	E......	E......	E......	E......	E......
S......	S......	S......	S......	S......	S......	S......

29	30	31				
W......	W......	W......				Shade in each day and feel free to use more than one colour for each day!
E......	E......	E......				
S......	S......	S......				

KEY

W - WEATHER
E - EXERCISE
S - SOCIAL

Sleep

Shade in the squares for each night and use the space below to record any relevant notes

HOURS →

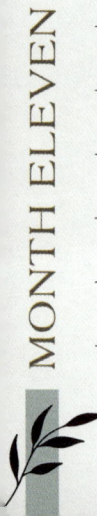

DATE

MONTH ELEVEN

SLEEP DISORDERS

Insomnia can affect us all. This is a sleep disorder where you can find it hard to fall asleep or stay asleep, or you wake too early, on a regular basis. Here are some tips if you're struggling to sleep

DON'T CLOCK WATCH
If you're lying awake in bed watching the clock, you're only going to start making yourself more stressed, which in turn will make it harder to sleep. If you can't sleep, or get back to sleep, in 30 minutes, get out of bed instead. Do something calming in low lighting, such as reading a book, and try again when you feel sleepy.

USE A JOURNAL
Stress and anxiety, as well as low mood, can be causes of insomnia. Try keeping a notebook by your bed and write down any worries at the end of the day as part of your bedtime routine. This can sometimes help the brain to relax and prepare for sleep rather than lying awake worrying.

EXPLORE EXTERNAL FACTORS
Insomnia can be caused by a lot of different factors, such as stress and anxiety, noise at night, too much light, a room that's the wrong temperature, discomfort or pain, shift work and so on. Try to eliminate any external problems where possible to see if it makes a difference.

SEE A DOCTOR
If you have tried to change your sleeping habits and you are still struggling to sleep after a couple of months, or if your insomnia is starting to affect your daily life and your moods on a regular basis, it's time to see a doctor to explore other options to help you sleep.

Diet & Nutrition

Tick the squares for each day of the month. At the end of the month, look at this page alongside the 'Monthly Overview' to see if you spot any patterns

DATE →

DATE	BREAKFAST	LUNCH	DINNER	2X HEALTHY SNACKS	VEGETABLES	FRUIT	GOOD FATS	PROTEIN	WHOLEGRAINS	AT LEAST 2 LITRES OF WATER	UNHEALTHY SNACKS	MORE THAN 4 CAFFEINATED DRINKS	ALCOHOL	VITAMINS/SUPPLEMENTS
1														
2														
3														
4														
5														
6														
7														
8														
9														
10														
11														
12														
13														
14														
15														
16														
17														
18														
19														
20														
21														
22														
23														
24														
25														
26														
27														
28														
29														
30														
31														

MONTH ELEVEN

GUT HEALTH AND MOODS

It's thought your gut bacteria produces 95% of your serotonin, which we know influences your mood, so it's worth making sure you have a happy tummy

FERMENTED FOODS

If you haven't tried fermented foods before, it's worth adding them in to keep your gut happy. Try things like kimchi, kefir, sauerkraut, live yogurt, tempeh and miso to see if you can reap the benefits of a more diverse gut microbiome.

FILL UP ON FIBRE

High-fibre foods have been shown to have a good impact on your gut health, so make sure you are getting plenty of fibre a day – many of us don't eat the recommended allowance of 30g per day. Try eating lots of beans, pulses, legumes, oats, bananas, berries and wholegrains.

Do you have an unhappy gut?
Tick the statements below that apply to you

- [ ] I REGULARLY SUFFER FROM GAS, BLOATING AND/OR HEARTBURN
- [ ] I OFTEN HAVE CONSTIPATION OR DIARRHOEA
- [ ] I CRAVE A LOT OF HIGH-SUGAR FOODS
- [ ] I OFTEN STRUGGLE TO SLEEP
- [ ] I SUFFER FROM ECZEMA, DRY SKIN OR SENSITIVE SKIN
- [ ] CERTAIN FOODS CAUSE ME TO HAVE DIGESTION ISSUES

All of these symptoms can be linked to poor gut health, so try improving your diet to see if it helps. If your symptoms are severe or long-lasting, do check with your doctor to rule out any underlying issues.

Physical Health

You can use words or emoji-style pictures to fill this bit in!

Keep track of your fitness for the month...

DATE	EXERCISE	HOW I FELT BEFORE, DURING AND AFTERWARDS

◇ How has your general physical health been this month? Any illnesses, injuries or aches and pains worth noting?

_____

_____

_____

MONTH ELEVEN

ILLNESS AND REST

We all get ill, injured or run-down from time to time. It's important to take the time to rest and recover to maintain your physical health

✳

LISTEN TO YOUR BODY

Sometimes physical health means rest not movement. Listen to your body and know when you need to stop for a bit to fully recover for a short period of time. You may need to stop activity completely, or you might need to adapt for a while. If you push yourself too hard, you could make your physical health worse, not better.

✳

ILLNESS AND MOOD

Being ill, injured or run-down can affect your mood, especially if you're used to being more physically active. It's normal to feel low when you're unwell, but remind yourself that taking time out is just as important and that it will support your goals in the long term. Just acknowledging this can help to boost your mood a little.

✳

Use this space to make a list of some self-care ideas you could try when you're feeling ill, injured or unwell, which you can refer back to if you need to take some time out from physical activity

_____

_____

_____

_____

_____

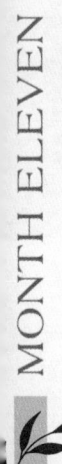

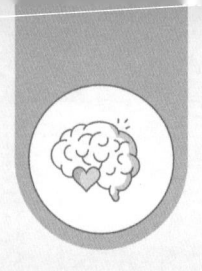

Mental Health

◇ Write down 5 things that have made you happy this month

_____
_____
_____
_____
_____

◇ Write down 5 things that have negatively impacted your mental health this month

_____
_____
_____
_____
_____

◇ What have you done to relax this month?

_____
_____

◇ What have you done to have fun this month?

_____
_____

MONTH ELEVEN

BEING GRATEFUL

Gratitude is another technique that can really help to boost your mental health and mood. We take a look at this practice

✦

MENTAL HEALTH BENEFITS

Gratitude is about being thankful for what we have in our lives. It's been shown that regularly expressing gratitude can improve your mood and give you a more positive outlook. It can also help you bond with other people by making them feel appreciated.

✦

MAKE IT ROUTINE

To get the best out of gratitude, it's best to be consistent with it. Why not make it a part of your bedtime routine? Or maybe you'd prefer to start your day with a mantra about what you are grateful for. Do whatever works for you and what you'll be able to stick to.

✦

What are you grateful for in your life right now?
It could be your physical health, people around you, your home – anything you can think of

_____

_____

_____

_____

_____

_____

_____

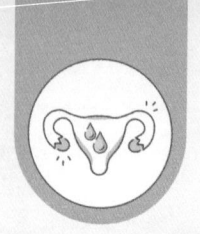

Menstrual Health

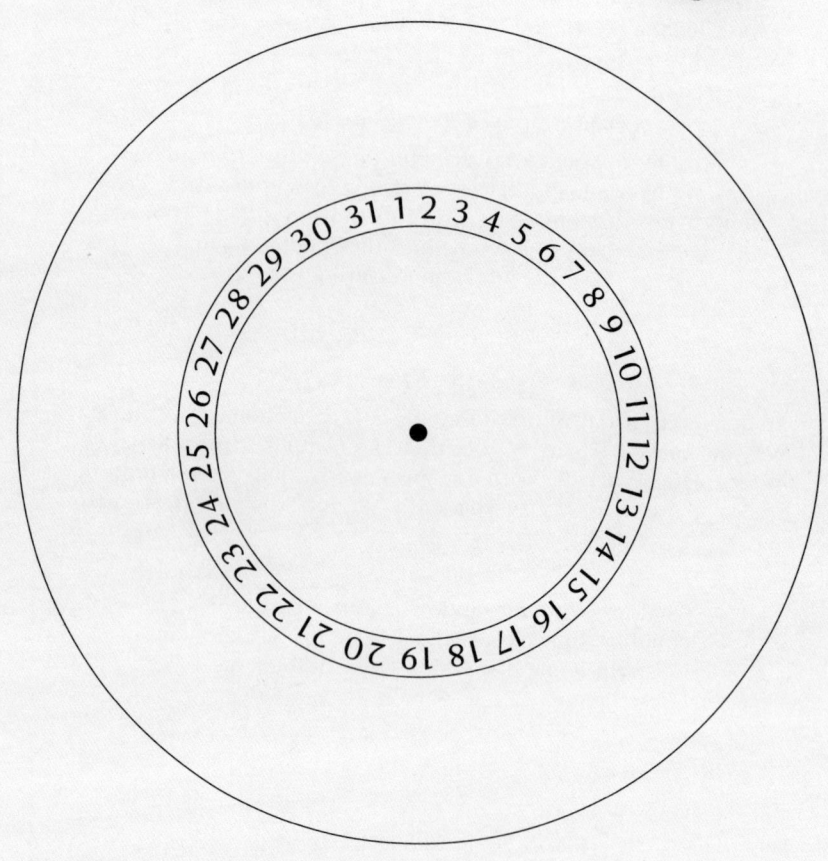

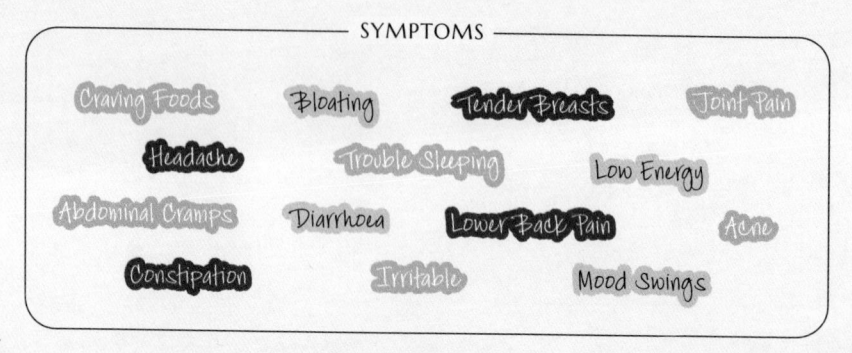

See page 7 on how to fill in the tracker

MONTH ELEVEN

---- SYMPTOMS ----

Craving Foods — Bloating — Tender Breasts — Joint Pain

Headache — Trouble Sleeping — Low Energy

Abdominal Cramps — Diarrhoea — Lower Back Pain — Acne

Constipation — Irritable — Mood Swings

PERIMENOPAUSE SYMPTOMS

Not sure if you're perimenopausal? If you're in your late 30s to early 40s, you might start to see some symptoms occur. Here are some of the most common symptoms...

Tick the boxes below if you experience any of these symptoms regularly

- ☐ IRREGULAR PERIODS
- ☐ ABNORMAL PERIODS (HEAVIER OR LIGHTER FLOW)
- ☐ HOT FLASHES OR NIGHT SWEATS
- ☐ BREAST TENDERNESS
- ☐ WEIGHT GAIN
- ☐ INCREASE IN PMS SYMPTOMS
- ☐ DECREASE IN SEX DRIVE
- ☐ VAGINAL DRYNESS
- ☐ CONCENTRATION OR FOCUS ISSUES
- ☐ THINNING HAIR
- ☐ MEMORY PROBLEMS
- ☐ MOOD SWINGS

If you tick quite a number of these symptoms, you might be entering the perimenopausal stage. You can still conceive during this stage, but it might be more difficult.

Sociability

◇ Who have you seen this month outside of your household and workplace? Make a note of how these interactions made you feel

PERSON	WHEN/WHERE	HOW IT MADE YOU FEEL

◇ Make a note of any days you've felt lonely

◇ Has anyone been demanding of your time this month? Make a note of how it made you feel

MONTH ELEVEN

YOUR SOCIAL PRIORITIES

On this page, you're going to consider your priorities when it comes to social events, to help you balance your social life better. Write down your thoughts below

✦

Social activities I want to prioritise going forward

_____
_____
_____
_____
_____

Social activities that are less important to me going forward

_____
_____
_____
_____
_____
_____

MONTHLY OVERVIEW

MONTH TWELVE

• Month _____   • Year _____

Notes

_____
_____
_____
_____
_____
_____
_____
_____
_____
_____
_____
_____
_____

1	2	3	4	5	6	7
W.........	W.........	W.........	W.........	W.........	W.........	W.........
E.........	E.........	E.........	E.........	E.........	E.........	E.........
S.........	S.........	S.........	S.........	S.........	S.........	S.........

8	9	10	11	12	13	14
W.........	W.........	W.........	W.........	W.........	W.........	W.........
E.........	E.........	E.........	E.........	E.........	E.........	E.........
S.........	S.........	S.........	S.........	S.........	S.........	S.........

15	16	17	18	19	20	21
W.........	W.........	W.........	W.........	W.........	W.........	W.........
E.........	E.........	E.........	E.........	E.........	E.........	E.........
S.........	S.........	S.........	S.........	S.........	S.........	S.........

22	23	24	25	26	27	28
W.........	W.........	W.........	W.........	W.........	W.........	W.........
E.........	E.........	E.........	E.........	E.........	E.........	E.........
S.........	S.........	S.........	S.........	S.........	S.........	S.........

29	30	31				
W.........	W.........	W.........				
E.........	E.........	E.........				
S.........	S.........	S.........				

KEY

W - WEATHER
E - EXERCISE
S - SOCIAL

Shade in each day and feel free to use more than one colour for each day!

Sleep

Shade in the squares for each night and use the space below to record any relevant notes

HOURS →

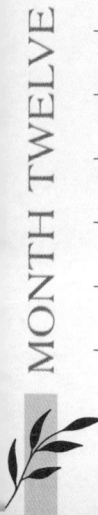

DATE ↓

	1	2	3	4	5	6	7	8	9+
1									
2									
3									
4									
5									
6									
7									
8									
9									
10									
11									
12									
13									
14									
15									
16									
17									
18									
19									
20									
21									
22									
23									
24									
25									
26									
27									
28									
29									
30									
31									

MONTH TWELVE

BEDROOM ENVIRONMENT

The room you sleep in and the bed you sleep on can impact on how much sleep you get, which in turn can affect your mood

PILLOW TALK

The right pillow can really make a difference to your quality of sleep. You want a pillow that is firm and comfortable, and one that holds your neck in a natural position to support your spine. If you often wake with a sore neck or back, it might be worth trying a new pillow.

ROOM MOOD

Colours and textures can influence your mood, and your bedroom is probably one of the most important rooms to consider. You want to ensure a calm, relaxing environment – ideally keep clutter to a minimum; use calm, neutral, pale colours; and focus on soft, comforting textures.

Use this space to draw your perfect bedroom – think about the colours and textures you find relaxing and calming

Diet & Nutrition

Tick the squares for each day of the month. At the end of the month, look at this page alongside the 'Monthly Overview' to see if you spot any patterns

DATE ↓

Date	BREAKFAST	LUNCH	DINNER	2X HEALTHY SNACKS	VEGETABLES	FRUIT	GOOD FATS	PROTEIN	WHOLEGRAINS	AT LEAST 2 LITRES OF WATER	UNHEALTHY SNACKS	MORE THAN 4 CAFFEINATED DRINKS	ALCOHOL	VITAMINS/SUPPLEMENTS
1														
2														
3														
4														
5														
6														
7														
8														
9														
10														
11														
12														
13														
14														
15														
16														
17														
18														
19														
20														
21														
22														
23														
24														
25														
26														
27														
28														
29														
30														
31														

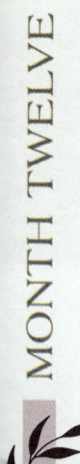

MONTH TWELVE

DELIGHTFUL DINNERS

Dinnertime can be a great opportunity to try new foods, experiment with recipes and spend time with your family. Make sure your meals are packed with mood-boosting ingredients for maximum benefit

BUILDING A MEAL

When you're thinking about what to have for dinner, try to build each meal around the essential macro nutrients: protein, carbohydrates and fat. Load up your plate with vegetables (at least half your plate) and try to get as many different-coloured veggies in your meal as possible.

TRY NEW RECIPES

We all get stuck in a food rut from time to time. Make an effort to experiment with new recipes, especially ones that feature mood-boosting ingredients. Why not set yourself a goal to try one new recipe a week? You can get the whole family involved in picking out new recipes to try.

Use this space to write down five new recipes you'd like to try that you haven't had a chance to make yet

1. _____
2. _____
3. _____
4. _____
5. _____

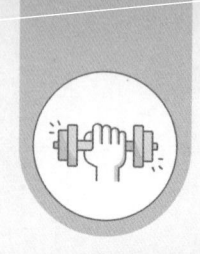

Physical Health

You can use words or emoji-style pictures to fill this bit in!

Keep track of your fitness for the month...

DATE	EXERCISE	HOW I FELT BEFORE, DURING AND AFTERWARDS

◇ How has your general physical health been this month? Any illnesses, injuries or aches and pains worth noting?

_____

_____

_____

MONTH TWELVE

COMMIT TO PHYSICAL HEALTH

You've worked hard on improving your physical health and now it's time to make a commitment to yourself that you will continue to support your health and moods going forward

✧

REMEMBER THE BENEFITS
If you find yourself wavering at any time, remember why you're going through this journey. You are looking to improve your physical health to ultimately lift your mood and make you feel happy, balanced and energised. Flick back through these Physical Health pages any time you need a reminder of how far you've come.

✧

MOOD AND PRODUCTIVITY
Your physical health can impact on lots of different areas in your life. By boosting your physical health, you can aid your day-to-day mood. Managing your mood has been shown to make you more productive at work, improve your relationships with friends and family, and boost your mental health.

✧

MY PROMISE
Use this space to make a promise to yourself and commit to your physical health. You can be as specific or general as you like – this is you writing to your future self

_____

_____

_____

_____

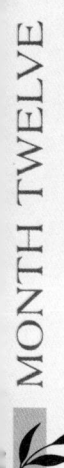

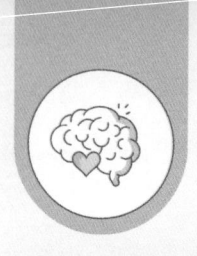

Mental Health

◇ Write down 5 things that have made you happy this month

_____
_____
_____
_____
_____

◇ Write down 5 things that have negatively impacted your mental health this month

_____
_____
_____
_____
_____

◇ What have you done to relax this month?

_____
_____

◇ What have you done to have fun this month?

_____
_____

MONTH TWELVE

GIVE TO OTHERS

Helping other people can be a big mental health boost
and improve your mood by making you feel good.
We have some ideas to get you started

VOLUNTEER

Volunteering is beneficial to society, but also to your mental health. It's been shown that giving your time to help others can help you feel happier, calmer and less anxious. It can also help with stress levels. There are lots of different types of volunteering, so do your research to find what's right for you. You don't have to commit to much – a couple of hours of your time will always be appreciated.

ACTS OF KINDNESS

Random acts of kindness are another way you can help others, while also benefiting your own mood and mental health. Why not give someone a call to see how they are, or gift someone a bunch of flowers, or help with a task that needs doing? These acts will make you feel good, as well as lift another person's mood too.

Do you have any ideas for how you can help other people?
Jot down a few bullet points here

_____

_____

_____

_____

_____

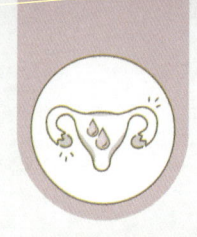

Menstrual Health

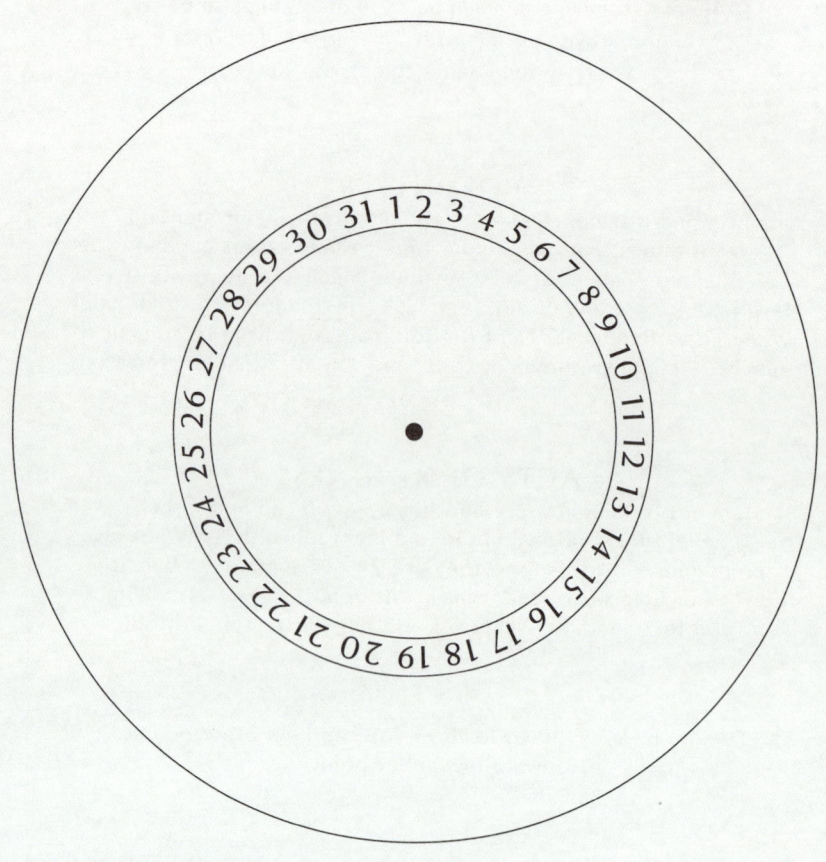

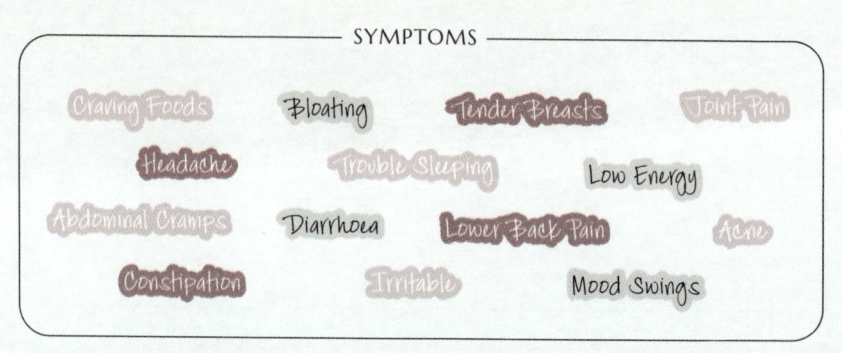

See page 7 on how to fill in the tracker

Tracker circle with days 1–31 around the inner ring.

― SYMPTOMS ―

- Craving Foods
- Bloating
- Tender Breasts
- Joint Pain
- Headache
- Trouble Sleeping
- Low Energy
- Abdominal Cramps
- Diarrhoea
- Lower Back Pain
- Acne
- Constipation
- Irritable
- Mood Swings

MONTH TWELVE

SELF-CARE DURING YOUR CYCLE

Be kind to yourself wherever you are in your menstrual cycle and take time to give yourself some TLC to manage your moods and lift your energy

✦

SKINCARE TIPS

Your fluctuating hormones can play havoc with your skin. During your period, use gentle skincare products as your skin can be more sensitive and prone to breakouts. After your period, when your oestrogen starts to increase again, you can look at repairing your skin with vitamin C-boosting face masks or creams, for example.

✦

ACHES AND PAINS

Our bodies go through a lot from month to month, so it's no wonder that we experience various aches and pains throughout our cycle. Treat yourself to a massage, a warm bath or by moisturising when you're feeling sore. Keeping on top of pain will help you to balance your moods too.

✦

Write down some of your favourite self-care activities here that help you during your menstrual cycle, and pick one when you're feeling sore, run-down or low

_____

_____

_____

_____

Sociability

◊ Who have you seen this month outside of your household and workplace? Make a note of how these interactions made you feel

PERSON	WHEN/WHERE	HOW IT MADE YOU FEEL

◊ Make a note of any days you've felt lonely

_____
_____

◊ Has anyone been demanding of your time this month? Make a note of how it made you feel

_____
_____

MONTH TWELVE

LEARN TO SAY NO

It can be hard to say no to certain events, but when it comes to looking after your moods and finding balance, learning to turn down invitations is key

POLITELY DECLINE

You don't need to give too much detail when you're saying no to an invitation. Make sure you reply sooner rather than later – don't stew over it for a long time or you will create more worry and anxiety. Explain that you're unable to attend in a polite manner and thank them for inviting you. You can simply say that you have other plans – even if those plans are a little self-care and alone time.

SUGGEST ALTERNATIVES

When you receive an invitation to an event that you don't feel comfortable attending (too many people you don't know, too far away or too big, for example), why not suggest an alternative for another time that suits your lifestyle better? If it's a friend you do want to see, you could say that you're sorry you can't attend but maybe you could catch up over coffee soon.

Draft a template reply here that you can use when you want to say no to an event or invitation. You can adapt it each time, but this will prompt you with what to say

_____

_____

_____

_____

_____

MOOD
·JOURNAL·

Future PLC Quay House, The Ambury, Bath, BA1 1UA

Editorial
Editor **Sarah Bankes**
Art Editor **Madelene King**
Compiled by **Alice Pattillo**
Senior Art Editor **Andy Downes**
Head of Art & Design **Greg Whitaker**
Editorial Director **Jon White**

Contributors
Julie Bassett & Sarah Bankes

Cover images
Shutterstock

Advertising
Media packs are available on request
Commercial Director **Clare Dove**

International
Head of Print Licensing **Rachel Shaw**
licensing@futurenet.com
www.futurecontenthub.com

Circulation
Head of Newstrade **Tim Mathers**

Production
Head of Production **Mark Constance**
Production Project Manager **Matthew Eglinton**
Advertising Production Manager **Joanne Crosby**
Digital Editions Controller **Jason Hudson**
Production Managers **Keely Miller, Nola Cokely,
Vivienne Calvert, Fran Twentyman**

Printed in the UK

Distributed by Marketforce, 5 Churchill Place, Canary Wharf, London, E14 5HU
www.marketforce.co.uk Tel: 0203 787 9001

Mood Journal Second Edition (LBZ5094)
© 2023 Future Publishing Limited

We are committed to only using magazine paper which is derived from responsibly managed, certified forestry and chlorine-free manufacture. The paper in this bookazine was sourced and produced from sustainable managed forests, conforming to strict environmental and socioeconomic standards.

All contents © 2023 Future Publishing Limited or published under licence. All rights reserved. No part of this magazine may be used, stored, transmitted or reproduced in any way without the prior written permission of the publisher. Future Publishing Limited (company number 2008885) is registered in England and Wales. Registered office: Quay House, The Ambury, Bath BA1 1UA. All information contained in this publication is for information only and is, as far as we are aware, correct at the time of going to press. Future cannot accept any responsibility for errors or inaccuracies in such information. You are advised to contact manufacturers and retailers directly with regard to the price of products/services referred to in this publication. Apps and websites mentioned in this publication are not under our control. We are not responsible for their contents or any other changes or updates to them. This magazine is fully independent and not affiliated in any way with the companies mentioned herein.

FUTURE Connectors. Creators. Experience Makers.

Future plc is a public company quoted on the London Stock Exchange (symbol: FUTR)
www.futureplc.com

Chief Executive **Zillah Byng-Thorne**
Non-Executive Chairman **Richard Huntingford**
Chief Financial and Strategy Officer **Penny Ladkin-Brand**

Tel +44 (0)1225 442 244

Widely Recycled

ipso. For press freedom with responsibility